HEAT
STROKE

Best of luck
in Australia!

Michael

MICHAEL G. SIMONSON

HEAT STROKE

Why Canada's Summer Olympic
Program Is Failing and
How We Can Fix It

Published by
BPS Books
Toronto, Canada
bpsbooks.com
A division of
Bastian Publishing Services Ltd.

ISBN 978-1-926645-07-0

Canadian Cataloguing in Publication Data available from Library and Archives Canada

Cover design: Angel Guerra, Archetype
Text design and typesetting: Tannice Goddard, Soul Oasis Networking

To my son Kale

*"Be who you are and say what you feel,
because those who mind don't matter
and those who matter don't mind."*
(ATTRIBUTED TO DR. SEUSS)

I love you so much!

Contents

Preface

Have you ever dreamed of the Canadian flag being raised in your honour at a major international sporting event? Most likely you have. In fact, the scene is imagined on a daily basis in backyards, arenas, and gymnasiums across Canada as young and old alike envision scoring that last-minute goal, skating the perfect program, breaking the world record, and in the process standing atop the podium while an adoring nation watches their every move.

For many it is just that, a dream, but for me it was a life that I lived and experienced as a carded athlete on Canada's national rowing team from 2001 to 2003. As the majority of Canadians rose from their nighttime slumbers and headed out the door for an honest day's work, I, like many other dedicated Canadian athletes across this great land, proceeded to my place of practice (for me a rowing venue, for others the local gymnasium, hockey rink, or track). My efforts were not fuelled by the prospect of money, notoriety, or fame but by a belief. A belief that if I devoted myself to my craft, if I obeyed my coaches' orders, then I could actually bring my dream to life.

However, the reality in Canada is that only one segment of this ever-so-small group of athletes truly has a chance of living out that dream. That segment is made up of our winter athletes, a fact that is discouraging to me as an alumnus, director, and coach in Canada's summer athletic system. Today, if your son, daughter, friend, or colleague aspires to stand on the Summer Olympic podium, unless they are one of the privileged few competing within the sports of rowing, equestrian, or women's wrestling, do them a favour: Tell them to quit now because not only do the results from the 2008 Olympic Games reflect the likelihood of summer failure, so do the actions of the country's sporting community.

This book argues, however, that all Canadian athletes — summer and winter alike — should be able to pursue their dream. With the 2012 Olympic Games now only a few years away, the time is now to put forth a plan that will elevate our country's summer athletic prowess.

Heatstroke invites you to step inside Canada's amateur sport system and find out why Canada's summer athletes suffered failure in Sydney, Athens, and, most recently, Beijing, and to see what we can do to make sure it won't happen in London — or ever again.

Acknowledgments

This book would not have been possible without the support of the hundreds of athletes, coaches, officials, and journalists in Canada's amateur-sport system who like me wish to restore Canada's sporting legacy at future Summer Olympic Games. A special word of thanks goes out to Jane Roos, whose support through this entire research and writing process was immeasurable. And to:

Donald G. Bastian and Arnold Gosewich, who guided me every step of the way in the writing and publishing of this book. My appreciation for your support goes beyond words.

My friends, colleagues, and co-workers who expressed an interest in my project, especially Nerissa Goodman, Sirkka Vandergraaf, Nicole Kolar, and Christina Fuller, who helped in editing the manuscript; Jon Lee, for his behind-the-scenes support; and my adopted family at the Calgary

Rowing Club and the Alberta Rowing Association. This project would not have come to completion without all of your support.

My wife, Lisa Simonson, and my parents, Vern and Donna Simonson, who have always encouraged me to follow my dreams. Thank you!

Introduction

At first glance, the 2008 Summer Games were a success for Canada. Eighteen medals represented our best performance at the Summer Olympics since 1996, demonstrating to many that Canada had turned the table on its Summer Olympic misfortunes. But a dose of reality is in order: The Games were a success only because of an improved medal count compared with what we achieved in Athens and Sydney — Games that themselves were abject failures.

In fact, when medals won are evaluated as a percentage of medals awarded, Canada won the same percentage of medals in 2008 as it did at the 1976 Games in Montreal, an Olympiad that most Canadians now see as a disappointment.

At the 1992 Games in Barcelona, Canada finished eleventh in the Summer Olympic medal count. In Beijing, Canada finished tied for nineteenth. At the 1996 Olympics in Atlanta, Canada held its own among the G8 countries, beating both Japan and Great Britain in the overall medal count. Twelve years later, in Beijing, we finished a distant last among G8 countries, winning

38 percent fewer medals than our next closest rival, Japan. Let the results from the 2008 Summer Olympics show that while Canada improved on its medal count from four years earlier, it has a long way to go if it wishes to compete with the world's sporting powers.

The contention of this book is that Canada's athletes can compete with the world's sporting powers at the Summer Olympic Games. We can hear our national anthem played over and over again as a good number of our summer athletes stand on the medal podiums. But first we must take a hard look at the good, the bad, and the ugly of our current sport system.

This book delivers a diagnosis of Canada's summer sporting ills from the federal government down to the athletes themselves, against the backdrop of the triumphs of our winter athletes. It pulls together inside knowledge of the challenges faced by athletes and summer sport organizations today. It reveals what is going on behind the doors of Canada's sport organizations. It shows how Canada's success at the 2006 Winter Olympics in Torino, Italy, and our prospects for success in Vancouver in 2010 are not the result of the federal government or the Canadian Olympic Committee, but rather of a sporting entity independent of both of these entities.

But *Heatstroke* not only provides an in-depth history and diagnosis of Canada's amateur sport system, it also examines Canada's plan for resurgence at the Summer Olympics, while offering its own blueprint for success, not just in the short-term but for many Olympiads to come.

Heatstroke compares Canada's plans for Olympic success with the Australian approach to Olympic ascendancy. Australia and Canada are alike in a striking number of ways, including form of government, size of population, and lifestyle. Australia, however, has created a sport system that benefits all of its athletes, and this is richly illustrated by their Olympic medal count. This book parses out how our Commonwealth cousin overachieves at the Summer Olympic Games and shows how we can emulate them.

Examining the ideas and concepts of high-ranking sport officials and athletes throughout the world, *Heatstroke* provides a made-in-Canada solution to our summer sporting ills. A number of steps are presented to Canada's newfound sport saviour Alex Baumann and the country's other organizers and officials, including elected politicians, for restoring our sporting legacy at the Summer Olympics while maintaining our present rate of success at the Winter Olympics. *Heatstroke* will show that many of these steps have already been implemented in Canada's winter sport system.

Running throughout the book is a portrayal of the career of a real Canadian Summer Olympic hero: Tracy Cameron, a rowing athlete in the women's lightweight double sculls who competed at the 2008 Summer Games in Beijing. I have had the good fortune to be Tracy's friend over the years, and am grateful to be able to share her story with you. You will experience her determination, frustrations, passion, and glory as she progresses from the Calgary Rowing Club to the Canadian national team to the Olympics.

Tracy is an idol of and inspiration to thousands of young athletes — the Tracys of the 2012, 2016, and 2020 Olympiads. Their success or failure will be determined by much more than their own raw talent or willpower.

As this book shows, real actions, taken by Canada's summer athletes and by the organizations that fund and train them, will decide whether our future athletes experience Olympic glory or defeat.

PART ONE

Why We Win at the Winter Olympics

1

A Nation Sinks Back in Disappointment — Again

Did you see it? At 4:30 a.m. Atlantic time, in the summer of 2008, an official sitting high above the start line at the Shunyi Olympic rowing-canoeing park, in Beijing, China, announced the entries for the women's lightweight double at the Olympic final for rowing.

All of Canada's rowing community, as well as millions of Canada's Olympic faithful followers, ceased whatever they were doing. In China, nearly forty-five thousand fans lined the course, and Canadian supporters painted in red and white chanted in unison while waving Canadian flags: "GO, CANADA, GO!" For the next seven minutes, the eyes of Canada's sporting world were focused on two individuals: Tracy Cameron and her lightweight doubles partner, Melanie Kok.

In the two-week lead-up to the Games, rowing — never a pursuit to spark much interest among Canadians — was written about and analysed more than at any time in recent history. Not since McBean and Heddle did Canada have a more dominant female duo in the rowing sculls. Prior to the Games, these two Canadian rowers were proving to be world beaters.

In Lucerne, Switzerland, their first international race together, they had finished third. Two weeks later, in Poland, at the last world cup event before the Games, they had won by more than four seconds. And at the Games themselves, the two were not letting up at all. In the Olympic semifinal they dominated their race, leading from start to finish — leaving some journalists to wonder if the real race wasn't for second place.

In Shubenacadie, Nova Scotia, her hometown, Tracy was idolized like few athletes before her. Well-wishers from surrounding towns rallied behind her. Local papers compared her with another rowing legend, Silken Laumann, and wondered if she might be the most dominant rower ever to hail from the province. School kids mailed letters of support and local sport organizations hung pictures of her in their offices.

On the morning of the race, Canada, some five thousand miles away, was cast in darkness. By four in the morning, the streets of adoring small towns throughout Nova Scotia and across Canada were deserted. Lobster fishermen busy preparing their morning traps turned off their fishing vessels and downloaded the race onto their laptops.

The sounds of the head race official floated out of the ocean bay and community bars, spilling onto city streets and regional roads. The competitors were announced: "Women's Lightweight Double Final: Netherlands ... Finland ... Canada ... Germany ... China ... Greece ..."

The question that nagged at us was whether we would sink once again back onto our couches, or into our cups, wondering why our Summer Olympians couldn't be more like their winter counterparts who fight, compete, and win with predictable regularity.

Failure certainly was the theme with most of the Canadian athletes at Beijing.

Brent Hayden was a world champion in the 100m freestyle at the 2007 World Aquatic Championships in Australia. At the Summer Games in Beijing, however, he failed to make it out of the semifinal, finishing a disappointing eleventh. In contrast, Chandra Crawford was relatively unknown heading into the Winter Games in Torino but came out of them as Canada's Olympic darling, bringing home gold in cross-country skiing.

Perdita Felicien was one of four Canadians who were world champions in their events heading into the 2004 Athens Olympics. Incredibly, all four failed to make it to the podium, with Felicien falling after crashing into the first hurdle in the women's 100m hurdles final. Again, in contrast, their winter colleague, Cindy Klassen, was a favourite to win three medals in Torino in 2006. When those Winter Games reached their conclusion, she in fact brought home five medals, becoming Canada's most decorated Olympic athlete of all time.

Looking farther back, to the men's 100m track and field final at the 1988 Olympics in Seoul, Korea, Ben Johnson brought an entire nation to its feet when he not only ran a world record time of 9.79 seconds but also defended the pride of our nation by beating Carl Lewis of the United States. Only to be followed by that moment of horror, when the results of his urine sample were broadcast around the world and he was stripped of his medal. Ross Rebagliati tested positive for a banned substance following his gold-medal performance in snowboarding at the 1998 Games in Nagano, Japan, but unlike Johnson, he retained his medal, becoming a Canadian hero upon his return home.

Olympic results from the past four Olympiads show that our winter athletes are nine times more likely to stand on the Olympic podium than their summer counterparts.

Looking for a scapegoat

Why are things this way? Is it because our athletes are inferior? Are they timid, choking when it matters most? Are sports secondary to our culture as Canadians? Are we a country that doesn't care about our Summer Olympians?

The answer to all these questions is a resounding no.

Our country has produced some of the greatest summer athletes in the world. Justin Morneau's performance during the 2006 regular season made him the MVP in Major League Baseball that season. Steve Nash was the 2005 and 2006 MVP of the National Basketball Association. Lennox Lewis was the Heavyweight Champion of the world. Alexander Despatie is a three-time world champion in the sport of diving. Alex Baumann and Victor Davis are former world record holders in swimming. At the 2007 World Rowing Championships, Canada's men's eights won the world title for the third time in the previous six years. Heading into the 2008 Olympics in Beijing, China, Adam van Koeverden was the defending World and Olympic Champion in the men's K-1 500m for kayaking.

And forget the charge of timidity. Brian Richardson, an Australian who coached Canada's national rowing teams from 1993 to 1996, and again from 2001 to 2004, once said, "Canadian athletes have that something extra that you don't see in other countries." Stories from our athletic heroes of the Torino 2006 Winter Games confirm his judgment.

When freestyle skier Deidra Dionne sustained a serious neck injury in a training run in September 2005, many thought she would never compete again. Yet she completed her remarkable recovery during the 2006 Olympics in Torino, competing in the women's aerials event. Or how about hockey player Joe Sakic? He competed in Torino with a broken jaw. Neither of these athletes won, but their efforts epitomized what it takes to compete at the Olympic level.

Courageous feats from our Summer Olympians show a similar resolve.

Silken Laumann won a bronze medal at the 1992 Olympics only ten weeks after a boat crashed into her lower right leg, exposing the bone. After the Olympics, Laumann took a year off from rowing to allow her injury to heal.

Carol Montgomery had hoped to become the first Canadian female to compete in two different sports at the same Summer Olympics — a surreal achievement for someone who nine months prior to the 2000 Games in Sydney was told she might lose her left leg because of a blockage in an artery. Montgomery was unsuccessful in her goal, but only because three cyclists crashed in front of her in the Olympic triathlon. She suffered a broken wrist and severe lacerations in the accident, forcing her to withdraw from her second event, the women's 10,000m in track and field.

Sport is definitely not incidental to the culture of Canada. From paddling canoes in Muskoka to playing hockey on frozen ponds across the prairies to sailing the thousands of miles of our three coastlines, we are involved in one of the widest ranges of sporting activities of any people in any one country. Sport is the one activity that unifies this country across six time zones, three oceans, two national languages, and a multitude of cultures.

Canada has played a major role in developing sport around the world. The country is known as the birthplace of ice hockey and lacrosse. Basketball was invented by a Canadian, Dr. James Naismith, as an activity to keep us busy during the winter. The Canadian Football League is the oldest football league in the world, and St. John's, Newfoundland, with its annual rowing regatta, is known as the host of the oldest continuing sporting event in North America. The sport of canoeing is attributed primarily to Canada. Even baseball, considered the quintessential American game, is reported to have been played first on Canadian soil, in 1838, seven years before Alexander Cartwright founded the New York Knickerbockers. Over the past 150 years, no other country in the world has had as great an impact on the creation of sport.

And we do care about our Olympians, whether winter or summer. Look no further than the fervour created by Canada's gold-medal-winning victory in hockey at the 2002 Olympic Games, and the excitement created by Donovan Bailey when he won the 100m in Atlanta. Both victories brought a nation to a halt and then sent happy citizens into the streets rejoicing. The names of Mario Lemieux and Donovan Bailey are now immortalized in Canadian culture, alongside those of Nancy Greene, Gaetan Boucher, Barbara Ann Scott, and Marnie McBean.

The winter-summer discrepancy

Why, then, all these memories of our winter athletes standing on the podium and summer athletes apologizing to the nation in hangdog media interviews?

In an ongoing case of national denial, we often float the idea that Canada is just a winter sports nation. Patricia Chafe, an official with the figure skating team in Torino, says our winter success makes sense because of our weather. "The Canadian public just loves winter sport," says Chafe. "These are things that are part of our lives for a good four to five months of the year." However, according to Statistics Canada, soccer, not hockey, has the highest participation rate in Canada, and swimming trumps figure skating.

Some suggest another idea: that Canadians don't care about summer sports. But this won't wash. The 2001 IAAF World Track and Field Championships in Edmonton were arguably the most successful world championships ever staged. Furthermore, the 2007 FIFA Under-20 World Cup of Soccer, which was hosted across Canada, set an all-time attendance record, surpassing the previous record set by soccer-mad Mexico some twenty-four years ago. Upon hearing of this achievement, FIFA president Joseph S. Blatter stated, "The way Canada has embraced this event is a testament to the strength and long-term potential of the sport of soccer (in Canada), as well as a reflection of the sporting passion in the heart of all Canadians."

Amateur sport is underfunded, some argue. We tell ourselves that if we want to be serious about sport, we have to start putting more money into it. But in the period from 2004 to 2010, the government of Canada will have devoted nearly $2 billion toward the country's Olympic movement.

Chris Rudge, the CEO of Canada's Olympic Committee, blames Canada's poor results at the Summer Olympics on the neglect of the 1990s. The results of cutbacks during that decade are just now coming to light, he says. "We lost the lottery money sometime in the eighties and there was a pretty serious recession in the late eighties and early nineties — and as investment fell off, that's where we saw a potential for a loss of results down the road." But how does Rudge explain the fact that Canada's performance has steadily improved over the course of the past five Winter Olympiads but has dropped dramatically since those Summer Games in 1996?

The fact is, Canada rarely does well at the Summer Olympics. A recent study by Andrew B. Bernard and Meghan Busse of Dartmouth University and the University of California at Berkeley, respectively, hypothesized that a country's medal total could be predicted by determining its GDP, population base, and host nation status. They found that, when taking these variables into account, Canada was one of only two nations (the other being Japan) that consistently underperformed on the Summer Olympic stage.

We hear that our athletic facilities are old and outdated but forget that Canada has hosted, since 1976, as many summer sporting events as Australia. Since that time Canada has hosted one Olympic Games, two Commonwealth Championships, one Pan American Games, the IAAF World Track and Field Championships, the FINA World Aquatic Championships, the Canada Games (every two years), and numerous other international events. Bob Storey, president of the International Bobsleigh and Skeleton Federation, acknowledges that Canada's high-performance sport infrastructure ranks right up there with the best in the world.

Flagging athletes and preening politicians

When all the excuse-making is said and done, and easily countered by the facts, we are faced with the stark reality that the decline of our summer athletes has been caused by the decline of our amateur sport system. And if not for the leadership and vision displayed by Canada's winter sport movement, the same would hold true of winter sports.

The 1988 Calgary Winter Olympics not only left a lasting imprint on the city of Calgary, it also created the foundation for the creation of a sporting institute where all of Canada's best winter athletes could train in one location. The organization responsible for maintaining the facilities from these Games, WinSport Canada, not only cares for the facilities' operational costs but also provides financial assistance to winter athletes and sport organizations alike.

WinSport Canada was originally founded in 1956 under the name of the Calgary Olympic Development Association (CODA), to win the right for Calgary to host an Olympic Winter Games. Following the 1988 Olympics in that city, the organization was restructured to leverage the legacy of the Games. The association's mandate was to ensure the continuing use of Olympic venues long after the Games were over. Committing the legacy of the 1988 Olympic Winter Games to the complete development of Canada's Olympic winter athletes and the organizations that serve them, CODA (now WinSport Canada) has evolved into one of the premier sport-development organizations in the world.

And so it is that we see Canada's winter sport organizations, backed by some of the best winter facilities in the world, follow WinSport's lead by hiring knowledgeable individuals who have helped develop Canada's most decorated athletes. The result is overwhelming international success.

Consider the sport of speed skating. Despite having North America's first indoor oval, Canada failed to win a single medal in long track speed skating at both the 1988 and 1992 Olympic Winter Games. At the 1994 Games in Lillehammer, Norway, Canada's speed skaters returned home with a silver medal, hardly the success we have come to expect today. Truthfully, it wasn't until 1995 that Canada's speed skating program began its resurgence. In 1995, with the assistance of WinSport and the Olympic Oval high-performance program, Speed Skating Canada hired external consultants and revamped its organization with the express goal of seeing Canada become the top speed skating nation in the world. In 2006, Canada's speed skaters achieved the association's goal, winning twelve medals at the Olympic Winter Games. Adding to this success, WinSport recently completed a $3-million facelift to the Calgary facility, further evidence of its determination to see future speed skaters from this country atop the podium.

Vancouver will soon play host to the 2010 Winter Games. Nobody wants Canada to host a Games and finish last. As a result, the federal government and the Vancouver Organizing Committee have committed $110 million to winter athlete programs heading into these competitions. Vancouver certainly was the catalyst of this funding, says Alex Gardiner, high-performance director of the Canadian Olympic Committee.

Meanwhile, Canada's summer athletes sit and wonder, "What do I get out of this investment?"

But something interesting is revealed about sport in general in our country when organizations like WinSport and that $110-million grant are factored out: a lack of accountability on the part of sporting organizations, as well as many other sporting ills. The first thing that becomes evident is how little the federal government and the Canadian Olympic Committee, self-described leaders of Canada's amateur sports movement, have done to enhance amateur sport in our nation.

The dollars available to our Olympians are being usurped by politicians and bureaucrats who are building platforms for their swollen egos. Documents obtained five months after the 2002 Olympic Games in Salt Lake City showed that Canadian cabinet ministers had spent more than $397,000 at the Games. This amount exceeded the annual budgets of many high-profile Summer Olympic sports that year, including the Canadian Weightlifting Federation ($315,000), Triathlon Canada ($265,000), the Shooting Federation of Canada ($123,000), the Federation of Canadian Archers Inc. ($83,000), and the WTF Taekwondo Association of Canada ($325,000).

With the Games seen as a plum trip for elected officials and bureaucrats, strange things happen to the infrastructure of sport.

The Canadian Olympic Committee sent more administrators and support staff (271) than athletes (267) to the 2004 Summer Olympic Games in Athens. And many of Canada's top athletes weren't even there, in spite of meeting the Olympic qualification standard for their respective sports.

Tyler Christopher, the silver medallist at both the 2005 World Track and Field Championships and the 2007 Pan American Games in the men's 400m, did not go. Why? Because of two arbitrary and unfair conditions that were imposed solely on Canada's Summer Olympians by the Canadian Olympic Committee. First, track and field athletes had to meet Canada's own qualifying standard, which was more stringent than the international standard. Second, they had to meet it before a self-imposed deadline of July 11, 2004. Christopher qualified — three days before the international deadline of August 9, but one month after Canada's deadline. Ironically, had he been subjected only to the international standard for his event instead of the more stringent Canadian standard, he would have met Canada's July 11 deadline.

Preening politicians are joined by coaches who seemingly lack accountability. Take the sport of athletics, for example. At the 2000 Games, Les Gramantik was head coach of what turned out to be one of the most disappointing Athletics Canada squads ever assembled. Instead of being asked to resign, he was asked to coach again. At the 2004 Olympic Games in Athens, track and field failed to win a medal for the second Olympiad in a row. That didn't keep Gramantik and Alex Gardiner, who had been head coach of Athletics Canada at those Games, from going on to loftier positions within Canada's athletic community. Following the 2004 Games, Gardiner was promoted to the position of director of international performance in charge of overseeing Canada's high-performance programs. And Gramantik? He was the head coach for Canada's track and field team at the 2008 Olympic Games, a team that failed to meet expectations for the third straight Olympiad.

Following the Games in Beijing, Athletics Canada, looking to improve upon its Olympic performances, came full circle. Gardiner was rehired as head coach while Gramantik returned as an assistant overseeing the sport's high-performance centre in Calgary.

What about the athletes that such coaches are training? They may be compared with people in Third World famines who never see a cent of the boatloads of money sent to them by Western nations. Government and public funding of Canadian sport is more than respectable, but not enough of it is getting to the athletes themselves. Winter and summer athletes alike live below the poverty line, despite the fact that the government invests billions into amateur sport. Regrettably, Canada's athletes seem content with how little they get and appear to be unwilling to do anything to address the problem, hurting not only themselves but also the prospects of athletes to come.

Compounding the problem is the fact that, because of the commitment of time and energy it takes to become an elite athlete, virtually all athletes in Canada have to survive for a period of time without any form of government income. High-ranking officials within amateur sport acknowledge this as a serious problem but appear unwilling to do anything about it. When asked how non-carded athletes were to be funded, Chris Rudge, the coc's chief executive officer, skipped around the issue, saying, "The (developing) athletes will be funding themselves through sponsorship." But if Olympic-medal-winning athletes like trampolinist Karen Cockburn, one of only five Canadians to medal at three separate Olympiads (2000, 2004, and 2008), can't find a sponsor, how can we expect developing athletes to do so?

It's a different story for winter sport. WinSport has put a plan in place to create a housing facility for Canada's winter athletes. The facility will be located in Canada Olympic Park, steps away from the Olympic facilities in Calgary, and will help ease the financial burdens of Canada's Winter Olympic athletes.

Meanwhile, summer sport executives pay lip service to the problem and continue to brazenly inform the public that our Summer Olympic program is turning the corner. That must be some corner, because they have been telling us this since the 2000 Olympic Games. Prior to the start of those Games in Sydney, Australia, Canada's chef de mission, Diane Jones Konihowski, spoke on the state of amateur sport in Canada. "Sport is in a better place now," she said. "Things have changed. We're not just talking the talk, we're walking the walk when it comes to athletes. We're doing a better job."

Some talk. Some walk. Canada finished the 2000 Games with a measly fourteen medals.

In Athens in 2004, Michael Chambers, president of the COC, said of Canada's summer sport program, "Whatever happens here, whether we fall a few medals short or win more than Sydney, will have nothing to do with what's happened in the last couple of years — that horse left the barn a long time ago."

Despite all the talking points and starry-eyed prophecies, Canada's summer sports program hasn't even reached the corner, much less turned it. Canada's performance at Summer Olympiads has diminished to a point where the Games of 2004 could in many ways be considered Canada's worst showing at a Summer Olympiad since 1972, when we finished eighteenth overall in the standings.

After the record-setting performance by our winter athletes in Torino, Canadians were again rhapsodically informed of a sport system that is at the very top in the world. Following those 2006 Games, COC vice president Walter Sieber was quoted as saying that Canada's athletes were walking taller than they've ever walked. However, Canada's performance in Torino has not rubbed off on our summer athletes. The 2006 Commonwealth Games, which were a preview of things to come in Beijing, showed just how far Canada's summer sport program had fallen. For the first time in the history of these Games, Australia won more gold medals than Canada's collective medal count in able-body events. (The Commonwealth Games are the only major Games to include disability events in the overall medal total.) In the process, Australia nearly tripled Canada's medal total.

What makes these results so disturbing is the fact that only twenty-five years ago, at the 1984 Olympic Summer Games in Los Angeles, Canada won more medals than Australia. Furthermore, we nearly beat the Aussies in overall medals only fifteen years ago at the Commonwealth Games in Victoria, British Columbia. Soberingly, in Beijing, Australia won fourteen *gold medals* compared with Canada's eighteen *total medals*.

Our Olympic prospects

Unfortunately, Canadian athletes are unlikely to get any breaks at the 2012 Games, in London, because relatively few new sports are going to be included. Canadian athletes do very well in totally new sports. Consider that at the

2008 Games seven of Canada's eighteen medals were in sports introduced at or after the 1996 Olympics: Canadians won medals in women's wrestling, triathlon, trampoline, and lightweight rowing. In those sports that are new to the Summer Olympic program, it's only a matter of time before the rest of the world catches up to Canada and takes away its medals.

It has already happened in synchronized swimming and beach volleyball. Canada was a world leader in the former when the sport was first introduced at the 1988 Games in Seoul. Carolyn Waldo made all Canadians proud, winning two gold medals (one in the singles and another as part of a duo with Michelle Cameron Smith). Canada's last Olympic medal in the sport of synchronized swimming was at the 2000 Olympics. John Child and Mark Heese helped popularize beach volleyball in Canada, winning a bronze medal at the 1996 Olympic Games in Atlanta. Canada failed to win a medal in this sport at the past three Olympiads..

The *Toque*, Canada's weekly humour magazine, recently commented that if Canada wants to be successful at the Olympics, we will have to start lobbying the International Olympic Committee (IOC) to keep introducing uniquely Canadian sports to the Olympic program. It goes on to remark, "Every time a new sport is added to the Olympic repertoire, Canada already has a marked advantage, because we have been playing it for years prior to its introduction on the world stage. It takes other countries a couple of years to figure out the nuances of the sport. By that time we've pocketed a few medals, and we're on to the next Canadian-flavoured sport." The *Toque* suggests that if Canadian sport officials want to win more medals at future Olympiads, they should lobby the IOC to introduce such sports as Frisbee golf.

But as Canada tries to find new ways to win medals at the Summer Games, our winter athletes appear to dominate in all of their sports. At Torino, Canadians won medals in ten of the fifteen Olympic winter sports — the most of any nation competing at the Games — while finishing third in total medals. Interestingly, sixteen of the twenty-four medals won by Canadians came out of Alberta, where WinSport directs most of its efforts.

Heading to Vancouver

In 2010, the eyes of the world will be focused on Vancouver. Expectations will naturally be high for the host country. After all, we won twenty-four medals in Torino and are on record with a goal of topping the medal count in the 2010 Olympics. Strong stuff for a country that has never won an Olympic gold medal on home soil, whether at Montreal in 1976 or at Calgary in 1988.

In the dramatic lead-up to the Vancouver Games, corporations from across Canada are paying billions to get their names affiliated with the Games. The federal government is spending over $600 million for the construction of Games venues. Furthermore, provincial and municipal officials plan to spend over $2 billion to prepare the province of British Columbia for the biggest sporting event Canada has ever hosted.

Before that, however, came the most politically motivated Olympic Games since the 1936 Games in Berlin and the largest sporting spectacle the world had ever seen.

In Beijing, Canadian athletes faced a host country that dominated from beginning to end, using the global exposure to assert their presence as a world power. Winning medals in a wide variety of sports, China finished the Games with fifty-one gold medals. Canada's gold-medal performances were limited to the sports of rowing, equestrian, and women's wrestling, sports whose competitive pool is relatively shallow. When it came to sports that featured a worldwide audience, such as cycling, gymnastics, boxing, soccer, basketball, volleyball, track and field, and swimming, Canadian athletes virtually disappeared.

But while Canada's gold-medal performances in Beijing were limited to a few niche events, there is proof that Canada can change its Summer Olympic fortunes and compete in all athletic disciplines.

For evidence of that, we need look no further than Canada's Winter Olympic program. Prior to 1988, Canada's Winter Olympians toiled in relative anonymity, winning no more than five medals at any given Winter Olympiad since 1936. Today, Canada's Winter Olympians are among the most decorated athletes in the world. As John Furlong, CEO of the 2010 Games, notes, "Canada's winter athletes now have the right to think of themselves as winners."

Today, this winning feeling appears to be limited to our winter athletes. Canadians seem content to have their country's efforts focused here. That would be one way to go, or we could swim against the current and revamp the country's sports system so it benefits all of our athletes. Doing the latter will require some work, but Canadians have never been known to back down from a challenge. In fact, challenges have defined us as a nation. In April 1917, at a terrible cost, Canadians took from the Germans a ridge that no other army had been able to seize and found in their dead and wounded and in their victory, an identity. "It was Canadians from the Atlantic to the Pacific on parade," Brigadier-General Alexander Ross, a battalion commander at Vimy, said later. "I thought then that in those few minutes I witnessed the birth of a nation."

Athletes must find their voice

To see the rebirth of a sporting nation, Canada's athletes need to lead the fight. Nearly thirty years ago, WinSport initiated change in Canadian winter sport by winning the bid to stage the Calgary Olympics. Now is the time for all Canadian athletes to step up and make their voices heard, to fashion a sport system that benefits themselves and their country, not only in the coming Vancouver Winter Games but in all Games, summer and winter, to come.

Fortunately, there is evidence that Canada's summer sport programs now have, in Alex Baumann, a leader who will put some backbone in our athletes, inspiring them to mount just such an effort.

In 2006, fifteen years after letting Baumann get away, Canadian sport officials announced that he was returning home to take over a program aimed at putting athletes on the podium at the Summer Olympics. Baumann smashed world records in both the 200m and 400m individual medley races to win Olympic Gold at the 1984 Games, but left Canada shortly thereafter because he hadn't been able to find a suitable job in his own country. He took his skills to Australia and became the executive director of the prestigious Queensland

Academy of Sport, helping his adopted country produce many of the world's elite athletes.

Baumann's hiring should demonstrate that Canadians are committed to changing their country's Summer Olympic sporting system. Further evidence is demonstrated by the federal government's decision to invest $72 million to help fund Canada's summer sports programs from 2008 to 2012. However, an effective leader and money are only the start of the process, something that Baumann himself recognizes. "One person coming in is not going to change the system," he said. "We still have a long way to go, but once you start getting success, when people believe that Canadians can win, as they did in Torino (at the 2006 Winter Olympics), then that instills confidence in the athletes themselves."

The revamping of Canada's Winter Olympic program proved that the success Baumann speaks of takes time and focus. However, with a managed commitment to sport in which we use all of our resources effectively, Canada can become a force not only in winter sports but in summer sports as well. As Furlong states, "We have all the ingredients to be the best."

2

The New Ice Age: Things Weren't Always This Way

Tracy Cameron came to the sport of rowing rather late in life.

She moved from Nova Scotia to Calgary in 1999 to pursue a master's degree in sport medicine. Although she had never touched an oar in her home maritime province, she longed for water and joined the rowing club sitting atop the shores of the Glenmore Reservoir, the only body of water the city of Calgary has to offer.

The connection between rower and boat is an almost magical one. Sitting barely three inches above the water's surface where only a thin layer of carbon fibre separated her from nature, she could feel the morning mist rising off the water and hear the swish of the water against the hull.

Tracy was smitten. Practising every day in front of an ever-observant crowd of hundred-year-old spruce trees, majestic mountaintops, and Calgary skyscrapers, she considered herself the luckiest girl on the planet. Her days were what she had dreamed of and all her worries were relegated to a boat slightly less than thirty feet in length.

Tracy's focus day in and day out was to propel her thirty-pound boat as fast as she could. The task was a difficult one. Blending grace with power was the only way to achieve optimal speed.

Tracy knew she had to be faster. Pulling her oars through the water with greater and greater power was critical for success.

But she also was learning that the sport wasn't just about brute force. She also had to be able to balance a boat barely wider than a shoebox through changing conditions of rain, wind, snow, and sun. The steadier and smoother she could get the boat to run through the water, the faster it went.

Mastery occurs when a rower brings skill and strength together. Racing down a 2000m racecourse, rowers will tax their arms, legs, lungs, and mind while trying to row up to forty-five strokes per minute. The goal is to focus inward and maintain a relaxed, almost robotic rhythm: every stroke the same, face motionless, oars in the water, oars out of the water. And all this while enduring a mind-numbing pain that few will ever comprehend.

Rowing requires an exceptional love if mastery is to be achieved. And mastery would come quickly for Tracy. An accomplished basketball player and outdoor enthusiast with an extensive athletic background, she picked up the sport quickly. Progressing steadily from novice rower to club athlete, she did the unthinkable. She won gold at the prestigious Royal Canadian Henley Regatta in St. Catharines, Ontario, in 2002, after little more than two years in the sport.

After seeing success come so quickly — and backed by a club with a storied past, having produced Olympians Bruce Robertson, Don Telfer, Michael Belenkie, Bryan Donnelly, and Heather McDermid — Tracy set her sights high. Add to the mix Blair Rasmussen, a coach with a long and accomplished history in the sport, and Tracy was a strong contender for a spot on Canada's national rowing team and a trip to the Olympic Games.

For the next seven months, Tracy and Blair worked hand-in-hand to set out a plan that would see her dream become a reality.

Tracy often found herself training alone, rowing more than 150 kilometres per week over twelve separate workouts. In the morning sun of the summer and fall, her solitary single dominated the shoreline of the Glenmore Reservoir. And in the winter months, when the reservoir turned to a frozen slab of ice, she could be found in a poorly lit concrete room, with only the ghosts of rowers past to keep her company. Here in the basement of the rowing club, she worked away on a rowing machine to prepare her for the summer months. In her spare moments, she took her workouts to the cross-country ski hill, where six-hour workouts soon became a weekly norm.

～

The headlines throughout the Games in Torino told the story. "Crawford Sprints to Gold," reported the *Toronto Star*. "Scott and Renner Give Canada a Big Boost at the Olympics with Gutsy Silver," proclaimed the *Toronto Sun*. "Lueders, Brown Claim Bobsled Silver," announced TSN's website. We read about it on a daily basis. Canadian athletes were winning medals. More medals than they had before, twenty-four in fact and a top-three finish at the Olympic Games, leading the website of CBC News to wonder if Canada was emerging as a Winter Olympic powerhouse.

Results from the 2007, 2008, and now 2009 world cup and world championship circuit show that they are. On the back pages of the sports section, after the ongoing hockey analysis, the football line, and the basketball write-up, Canadians will read how their winter athletes are dominating the international scene.

Canada's downhill skiers, led by Eric Guay, Jan Hudec, Francois Bourque, John Kucera, and Britt Janyk, have become a force that is feared the world over. Pierre Lueders on the bobsleigh track is a two-time Olympic medallist and is demonstrating to the world that a third Olympic medal in Vancouver is a distinct possibility. Melissa Hollingsworth Richards, Michelle Kelly, Jeff Pain, and Jon Montgomery are flexing their muscles on the skeleton track. Cross country skier Chandra Crawford is back training full time, looking to defend her Olympic gold medal in 2010. Freestyle skier Jen Heil is demonstrating that her 2006 Olympic gold medal was no fluke by winning world cups the world over.

Canada's men's and women's hockey teams both returned home from overseas as world champions in 2007. Brad Gushue and his Olympic gold-medal-winning rink from Newfoundland failed to qualify for the 2008 and 2009 world championships, but don't think Canada's curlers have fallen. In fact, quite the opposite: Gushue's rink lost to eventual world champion Kevin Martin and his team from Alberta at the 2008 and 2009 Canadian curling play downs. And in figure skating, Patrick Chan again demonstrated Canada's prowess in the sport with a silver-medal-winning skate at the 2009 ISU World Figure Skating Championships in Los Angeles, California.

Canada's Olympic history

It would be easy to conclude that Canada has a long, prosperous history in winter sport. But truthfully, things were not always this way, which is surprising for a country where snow and ice cover a significant part of the landscape twelve months a year.

In fact, looking back some eighty years ago at the 1928 Games in Amsterdam, Canada was considered a Summer Olympic powerhouse. Winning fifteen medals in 109 events, Canada finished the 1928 Games ranked tenth in terms of total medals. Our athletes were some of the most successful the Games had ever seen. Percy Williams, a twenty-one-year-old from British Columbia, won not only the men's 110-yard dash but also the men's 220-yard event. In the process, he became the first and one of only two non-Americans (Usain Bolt of Jamaica being the other) in Olympic history to sweep both events. His feats were all the more remarkable for a man who weighed just 125 pounds and who fought through rheumatic fever as a child.

These same 1928 Games marked the first time that women were allowed to compete in the sport of Athletics — and the last time a Canadian woman won Olympic Gold in track and field. Canadian Ethel Catherwood won gold in the women's high jump, while Ethel Smith, Fanny Rosenfeld, Myrtle McGowan, and Florence Bell set a world record in winning gold in the women's 4x110-yard relay.

As Canada's summer athletes were enjoying Olympic stardom, it was Canada's Winter Olympians who were struggling to find the mark. The 1928 Winter Games in St. Moritz, Switzerland, were the first to be held in a different nation than the Summer Olympics the same year. (The 1924 Games had been held in Chamonix, France, as part of what was deemed a winter sports week and what are widely considered the first Winter Olympic Games. Up to 1920, winter sport events were contested as part of the Summer Olympic schedule.) At the 1928 Games, Canada managed to find the podium only a single time, that medal coming in the sport of ice hockey, with the University of Toronto Varsity Blues winning gold.

Canada's winter fortunes changed at the Games in 1932. Faced with major obstacles as a result of the Great Depression, less than half the number of athletes who had competed in St. Moritz attended the Games in Lake Placid, New York. Canadian athletes experienced phenomenal success, as a result, winning one gold, one silver, and five bronze medals. Canada won its first Winter Olympic medals outside the sport of hockey, while continuing its supremacy within the national pastime. (The Winnipeg Hockey Club won gold this time, marking the second time a hockey team from Winnipeg won Olympic Gold. The Winnipeg Falcons won in 1920.)

The Depression affected the Summer Games that year in much the same way. With many countries and athletes unable to pay for the trip, the 1932 Olympics in Los Angeles saw fewer than half the number of participants of the 1928 Summer Games in Amsterdam. Canada's performance, however, was again a memorable one, with our athletes winning fifteen medals.

Phil Edwards, winner of the bronze medal in both the 800m and 1500m events in track and field, was our most decorated athlete in Los Angeles and held the distinction of being the country's most decorated Olympian until his death in 1971. Christened the "Man of Bronze," having won five Olympic bronze medals, Edwards was also the first-ever winner of the Lou Marsh Trophy as Canada's top athlete, and the first Black Canadian male to win a trophy at what are now known as the Commonwealth Games. No Canadian male has won an Olympic medal in a distance event over 800m in the sport of track and field since Edwards did so in 1932.

As much as we can look back with pride at Canada's success at both the Winter and Summer Games in 1932, that year signified the end of Canada's sporting supremacy at the Olympics. It marked the last time that both Canada's Summer and Winter Olympic programs would finish within the top ten of the medal count in the same Olympic quadrennial.

Following Canada's third-place performance in Lake Placid, it took over seventy-four years before we would again achieve a top-three finish in the overall medal count of a Winter Games.

More disappointing is the fact that, from 1968 to 1988, we finished only once within the top ten of the Winter Olympic medal count.

Canada's Winter Olympic programs reached a new level of apathy during the 1960s, 1970s, and early 1980s, with Canadian athletes capturing only two gold medals from 1964 to 1980: Nancy Greene's win in alpine skiing at the 1968 Games in Grenoble, France, and Kathy Kreiner's win in the same sport at the 1976 Games, in Innsbruck, Austria.

There were moments during the rest of the 1980s when it appeared that Canada's athletic fortunes were beginning to change, but the country's hopes were quickly dispelled. In 1984, Gaetan Boucher's performance in Sarajevo, Yugoslavia, where he won three Olympic medals, showed signs that Canada was becoming a speed skating force. Four years later, Canada's speed skaters failed to win a single medal.

As for the Summer Games, the 1932 Olympics in Los Angeles marked the last time Canada would crack the top ten in a non-boycotted Games. In 1984, fifty-two years later, Canada had its best Summer Games ever-winning forty-four medals, leading some to believe that Canada's sport programs had turned the corner. However, Canada's performance at the 1988 Olympics in Seoul, South Korea, quickly squelched these hopes. Canadian athletes won a disappointing ten medals, confirming fears that Canada's successes in Los Angeles were the result of the Soviet-led boycott that saw most Eastern European nations stay home.

Truthfully, it wasn't until the 1992 Games, in Albertville, France, that Canada's fortunes appeared to change — but only in winter sports. Canada had a breakthrough performance at these Games, winning seven medals, our best finish in the overall medal count at a Winter Games in over thirty-two years. It was at these Games that Canada's winter athletes started a trend by which they would improve on the country's performance at each successive Winter Olympiad, a trend that has continued right up to the Vancouver 2010 Games.

In 1994, in Lillehammer, Norway, Canada improved on its performance in Albertville, winning thirteen medals. Some four years later, in Nagano, Japan, Canada won fifteen medals and cracked the top five in the overall medal count for the first time in over sixty-six years. At the 2002 Winter Olympics in Salt Lake City, Canada's winter athletes won seventeen medals, finishing fourth in the overall medal count. And then, in 2006, Canada finished within the top three of the overall medals count for the first time since its historic performance in 1932. But just as impressive as Canada's medal tally in Torino is the fact that Canada had thirteen fourth-place finishes and forty-five top-five finishes. Furthermore, Canada won medals in ten of fifteen disciplines, more than any other country at the Games. Unfortunately, Canada's performance at recent Olympiads has shown that its success is limited to its winter athletes. Canada did finish eleventh in the overall medal standings at the 1996 Games in Atlanta. Ever since that time, however, Canada's performance in summer athletics has continued to crash down a slippery slope.

Canada finished the 2000 Games in Sydney with a disappointing fourteen medals. At the 2003 Pan American Games in the Dominican Republic, Canada failed to win more medals than Cuba for the first time since 1995, while winning only five more medals than Brazil. In the final moments leading up to the 2004 Games in Athens, only two Canadian athletes in the sports of swimming, boxing, and track and field were ranked in the top five of their respective sports, and these athletes failed to win an Olympic medal.

Canada's summer athletes hit an all-time low at the Athens Games. Canadian athletes failed to win medals in track and field, swimming, boxing, and men's wrestling for the first time in over fifty years. And now, after the conclusion of the 2008 Beijing Games, we see that while our medal count has increased, little has changed. Consider that at the 2008 Games Canada's only multiple medallist was greatly assisted by a horse, Hickstead, who propelled rider Eric Lamaze to both gold and silver. If we factor out the performances of our four legged athletes, we see that the medal haul from the Beijing Games is on par with Athens and Sydney.

The winter phoenix

As we head toward the 2012 Games in London, it is apparent that Canada's summer athletes are operating in relative obscurity next to their winter counterparts. They are rarely talked about in the community newsletter let alone the local paper, falling further and further into oblivion. Canada's swimming team brought home a medal from Beijing. Our rowers and kayakers continued to flex their athletic muscles, winning a combined six Olympic medals. But stand back from the water's edge and you will see that Canada's Summer Olympic program is heading toward a medals drought in 2012. The hope, in basketball, volleyball, soccer, field hockey, water polo, and handball, is just to *qualify* for the Olympics, never mind win a medal. The likelihood of Olympic success in badminton, table tennis, fencing, weightlifting, modern pentathlon, archery, men's wrestling, and shooting is so small that even Canada's sporting brass has given up on entering athletes in these events. And one can only hope that boxing and cycling don't implode before the lighting of the Olympic cauldron in London.

How is it that after seventy years of similar results, our Winter Olympic program is now successful while our Summer Olympic program is crashing and burning? Why is it that only one Olympic program is transforming itself when both operate within the same system?

As the next chapter shows, the answer to this question is not at all a mystery. Canada's resurgence at the Winter Games really began in 1955, with the creation of the Calgary Olympic Development Association (later renamed WinSport Canada).

3

Rocky Mountain High: The Calgary Experience

After spending most of her free time around the Calgary Rowing Club in 2003, Tracy had progressed to become one of Canada's elite rowers.

A change of scenery was what she sought. With the waters of the Glenmore Reservoir frozen for another three months, Tracy packed her belongings, quit her job, and relocated to Canada's rowing capital in Victoria, British Columbia. It was time to make rowing her full-time profession.

But "profession" was a relative term. Tracy earned less than $2000 a year, paid for by her provincial sport association and the generosity of her home club. She worked odd jobs and relied on family and friends to help pay the bills. To cut down on expenses, she rode her bicycle everywhere and found herself sleeping on couches and floors in one-bedroom apartments across the city.

Unfortunately, not long after her arrival at Canada's national rowing centre, it became obvious to Tracy that she didn't belong there. Failing to impress Canada's rowing brass, she was asked to train outside the centre. She found herself in limbo: too fast to compete in a club environment but not fast enough to train with Canada's best.

With little access to coaching, she continued on, seeking the advice of anyone who had time to watch and give her some technical guidance. She sought out additional practice times and befriended national team coaches and team athletes whenever a free moment presented itself. All in the hopes of being granted the chance to train within the rowing centre.

Her dream never wavered. Week after week, she understood that getting to the Olympics was more about process than dream: the process of enduring when times are tough and support is seemingly non-existent. In spite of little outside support in Victoria, and therefore little opportunity to show her stuff, Tracy persevered through those initial months. Then Rowing Canada's top brass invited her to participate in the weekly time trial on Saturdays during which Canada's national rowers raced against the clock to see where they ranked against one another. Tracy made it a point to be prepared for each and every Saturday session, monitoring her development relative to Canada's elite.

Using the weekly time trial results as her motivation, Tracy slowly scaled Rowing Canada's walls. By May 2003, she was getting close to the top of those walls. A month later, she was invited in, to compete for a seat on the team going to the Pan American Games.

But being invited to compete for a seat and making Canada's National Rowing Team were two totally different matters.

∼

In 1955, with the goal of bidding for the 1964 Winter Games, a group of sportsmen in Calgary created an organization that would transform winter sport in this country.

While that organization, the Calgary Olympic Development Association (CODA), was unsuccessful in its initial bid, losing out to Innsbruck, Austria, the organization remained in existence. CODA bid again for both the 1968 and

1972 Winter Games, losing to Grenoble, France, and Sapporo, Japan, respectively. Little was heard of CODA for a few years following its failure to land the 1972 Games. In 1979, however, the organization was resurrected, to bid for the 1988 Olympics. On September 30, 1981, in Baden-Baden, West Germany, the International Olympic Committee finally recognized the merits of staging the Winter Games in Canada.

The timing was perfect. Calgary benefited enormously from marketing initiatives implemented by the Los Angeles Organizing Committee for the Summer Games in 1984. Using money paid by ABC and Olympic sponsors, the Calgary Organizing Committee built state-of-the-art athletic venues that could withstand the warm Chinook winds that blow across the Rocky Mountains in the winter months. The result?

North America's first indoor speed skating rink; Canada's first major arena capable of hosting international hockey matches on standard international ice; the country's first — and up to 2008 only — full-length bobsleigh/luge track, with its own ice-making facility; its first and only ski-jumping facility (as of 2007), available almost year-round; and a world-class ski hill.

This legacy of 1988 has transformed winter sport in Canada. Following the 1988 Winter Olympic Games, CODA, which would later evolve into WinSport Canada, was given the responsibility of managing the Calgary Olympic facilities. Calgary has since become the Mecca of training for Canada's winter athletes, fulfilling the wishes of the city's Olympic brain trust, who had hoped that Calgary's investment would make it the training grounds for future Winter Olympians.

Consider that of the 156 Canadian athletes who competed at the 2002 Winter Games, 85 of them were from Alberta. At the 2006 Torino Games, over half of the Canadian team trained in, or were from, Alberta, and for good reason.

Take sliding sports, for example. At Canada Olympic Park (COP), not only do Canada's bobsledders have access to Canada's only full-length bobsleigh/luge track, they also have access to a number of support services that no other city in Canada can rival. Bill France, vice president of sport for WinSport Canada, notes that COP offers in one location all the services that bobsledders/lugers and skeleton racers require. Meeting rooms, weight-training facilities, housing facilities, and regeneration rooms complete with hot-tubs, pools, and Jacuzzis are all within a five-minute walk of each other. Athletes from all three sports have access to a variety of specialists ranging from sport psychologists to nutritionists. And WinSport created two separate weight rooms at COP to satisfy the unique muscular requirements of each sport.

A little more than a ten-minute drive from COP is the Olympic Oval, on the University of Calgary campus. The Oval is home to arguably the world's fastest ice surface, one that has contributed to the fall of 125 world records and the rise of more than 40,000 personal best times since 1988. Athletes who train at the Olympic Oval have access to a high-performance weight room, laboratory testing, U of C sport medicine, regeneration and massage therapy, physiological assessment, and countless other services.

An hour's drive west on the Trans Canada highway is the newly refurbished Canmore Nordic Centre, the site of cross-country skiing during the 1988 Winter Games and current home of Canada's cross-country ski team. Athletes training in Canmore have access to every imaginable service needed for competing on the world level.

As John Mills, a former president of the organization, explains, WinSport is responsible for improving Canadian athletes.

While state-of-the-art athletic facilities dot the Calgary landscape today, there was a time during the 1990s that WinSport drifted from its mandate of maintaining the facilities from the 1988 Games. WinSport's Bill France notes that cutbacks in funding from the federal government during the 1990s got WinSport into the business of sport, assisting sport organizations with their funding needs through direct financial grants. But, as France explains, this new approach was not working, "The facilities were getting old, and we quickly realized that we had to follow our mandate and provide for sport. Now, instead of providing grants to sport organizations, we provide sport organizations with world-class facilities that meet their needs."

Gordon Ritchie, chairman of WinSport from 2008 to 2010, confirms this mandate. "We are now focusing on what we are good at, providing Canada's athletes with the best facilities in the world," he says. WinSport does so by investing in a number of multi-million-dollar projects that are benefiting Canada's athletes as they prepare for 2010. Recently implemented projects include a $3-million facelift to the Olympic Oval facility, an upgrade of its heating and ventilation system, and a $2-million expansion to the Bill Warren Training Centre in Canmore. But WinSport isn't just maintaining the facilities from the 1988 Games. They are also creating new facilities based on the requirements of Canada's winter sport organizations.

France notes that by maintaining contact with every winter sport organization, WinSport has an advantage over virtually every other sport provider in Canada. It understands the needs of Canada's winter athletes. "We are right there talking to the athletes, listening to their needs on a daily basis, and hearing what they want. We can't always provide it for them, but we listen. For example, snowboarders said they wanted a half-pipe that would resemble the facility at the 2010 Games. WinSport has now paid for such a facility." In 2007, Canada Olympic Park underwent a $3-million facelift and now houses a half-pipe that replicates the one to be found on Vancouver's Cypress Mountain for the 2010 Games.

As France points out, this level of communication is seamless. WinSport has four liaisons whose sole job is to listen to and accommodate the requests of Canada's winter sport organizations. If someone from a winter sport wants or needs something, all they have to do is call their liaison. If the liaison can't provide an immediate answer, WinSport will find someone who can.

Through this process, WinSport has created a number of winter sport facilities that give Canada's winter athletes access to top-level training facilities almost year-round. Not the least of these is a $4.2-million year-round, indoor, push-start training centre for sliding sports that allows Canada's athletes to practise their starts twelve months a year. Farnham Glacier, a $2-million ski hill funded by WinSport, allows Canada's ski and snowboard teams to train at home in Canada during the months of July and August, instead of having to travel to Europe and fight crowds on a shrinking glacier. Haig Glacier, a seasonal training camp operated by WinSport since 1989, allows Canada's elite cross-country skiers to train during the summer months.

And now, with visions of grandeur in 2014, WinSport is undertaking construction of a $276-million ice house, to be the new home of both Hockey Canada and Skate Canada. With four rinks for hockey and skating, a curling rink, a six-court gymnasium, and all the associated technical, human, and research services, the complex is exactly what athletes require to become Olympic medallists.

Understanding the needs of those they serve, WinSport is constantly looking at new ways to help Canada's amateur athletes achieve Olympic success.

In 1994, WinSport determined that half of its high-performing athletes were either dropping out of high school to pursue sport or leaving sport to pursue academics. Recognizing the problem, the organization joined forces with the Calgary Board of Education and developed the National Sport School, providing grade nine to twelve students with a flexible learning environment in which they can train and compete while keeping up with their studies. This vision makes John Mills, former president of WinSport, swell with pride. "Twenty of the 195 athletes, or over ten percent of the total team in Torino, were either graduates (of) or students at the National Sport School," he says.

Another important factor to consider is the location of the facilities managed by WinSport. Located at nearly 3,500 feet above sea level, Calgary has the highest elevation of any major metropolis in Canada, giving a physiological advantage to those who train there.

It is little wonder that Calgary and WinSport are developing athletes who are synonymous with winter excellence.

Chinook winds

Twenty years after CODA (WinSport) was anointed with managing the legacy of the Calgary Games, athletes based in the Stampede City are suddenly dominating on the international scene. Athletes who trained in Calgary or Canmore, Alberta, earned 66 percent of the medals won in Torino. Pierre Lueders and Lascelles Brown won silver in the men's bobsleigh after honing their skills on the Canada Olympic Park bobsleigh track. As Lueders said in a CBC News interview posted on the Internet, "Just having the facility in your own backyard where you can have world cups, whether it's men's or women's skeleton, ... keeps the sport in the public eye." This, he says, "can only be good in terms of keeping athletes interested and getting new athletes interested to come in."

With Cindy Klassen's five medals leading the way, Canada's long track speed skaters who train year-round at the Calgary Oval won eight medals in Torino. Following the Games, Mark Greenwald, then director of the Olympic Oval, spoke of how Calgary-based athletes became successful. "The foundation was forged when the facilities were built, and without the major capital investment twenty years ago, none of this would be happening," he said.

In Torino, the cross-country ski team of Beckie Scott and Sara Renner won silver in the team sprint, while Chandra Crawford won gold in the women's sprint. All three used the Canmore Nordic Centre as their home training base. Upon her retirement in 2006, Scott acknowledged the impact of WinSport on her career. She expressed her deep appreciation to that organization and Cross Country Canada as her "long-time supporters and partners in sport." She added that their long-term investment in sport "enabled myself, my teammates, and the next generation of elite racers to achieve greatness."

Not to be forgotten is the gold-medal-winning women's hockey team, which is based in Calgary at Father David Bauer arena, the home of Hockey Canada.

And now Canada's alpine team, who are able to train on WinSport's recently developed ski facility on Farnham Glacier, has joined in on the success. At the 2009 FIS Alpine World Ski Championships, John Kucera became the first Canadian man to win gold, doing so in the men's downhill. His feat proved that WinSport's investment appears to be paying huge dividends. Says CAST Alpine director Dusan Grasic, "It has always been my dream that we would have our own facility and we would be able to actually train on a very challenging downhill course right here in Canada before the start of the ski racing season. Unlike in Europe, we will have this whole place to ourselves. I don't think any nation in the world has that option or advantage."

WinSport's winning ways

Some are sceptical of WinSport's impact on Canada's success. They point instead to the Canadian ski-jumping program, whose facilities fell into disrepair until the Alberta government came to the rescue in 2005, allotting $600,000 to ensure that the program could continue at Canada Olympic Park. But as Gordon Ritchie, chairman of WinSport, explains, investing millions of dollars on a facility that is used by a limited number of athletes and has no inclination to host a world cup event is not a sound financial decision. Furthermore, if not for WinSport's efforts, the facility would be obsolete today. As it is, more than one hundred thousand runs on the 30m, 50m, and 70m ski jumps continue to take place at Canada Olympic Park each summer. And though the 90m ski jump has been rendered obsolete by ski-jumping technology, there is little doubt that WinSport's remaining facilities and support services are cutting edge, leading to the development of Canada's and the world's best Winter Olympians.

Careful not to rest on its laurels, WinSport continues to listen to Canada's athletes on a daily basis, using the information it gleans to develop world-class venues and produce future Olympic champions. With the 2010 Olympics in Vancouver, WinSport is working to become a Winter Olympic training ground for all of Canada's winter sport organizations. "The goal for us is to have all fifteen Winter Olympic sports housed right here," France said in an interview with the *Edmonton Journal*. "As long as they are here, they've got all the services they need. It is one-stop shopping. World-class facilities and all the support, medical, sport science, training, nutrition — everything will be on-site so they can get all their work done right here."

4

A Klassen Act: Canada's Speed Skating Success Story

At 145 pounds, Tracy was fifteen pounds above the cutoff weight for the lightweight class. Yet she didn't look the part of a heavyweight rower, either. With well-defined arms and a slender build, she was slimmer and fitter than most heavyweight women in the sport.

Her choice to compete as a heavyweight had always been straightforward. She had dominated the club scene as a heavyweight, and the thought was that she would continue to do the same as a high-performance athlete on Canada's National Rowing Team.

In Victoria, however, Tracy often found herself competing against women three inches taller and forty-five pounds heavier than she. She was a girl competing against women, giving up a considerable amount of power to her competitors. Despite her obvious technical superiority, she could never make up for the obvious size differential.

After failing to make Canada's national team in 2003 and 2004, she returned home to Calgary, looking to re-evaluate her situation. The medical professionals whose advice she sought convinced her that she could lose fifteen pounds and compete as a lightweight rower.

It was a risky proposition. Not only would she be attempting to transform her body — a body that didn't have much extra weight to lose — but there were only two available seats per country in lightweight women's rowing at the Olympic Games.

Lightweight women's rowing, first introduced to the Olympic movement in 1996, was designed to give rowing a more universal appeal. Eastern European and Western countries were dominating rowing. The sport needed a way to give smaller-stature athletes — most notably from Asian countries — an opportunity to be competitive.

Restricted to women under 130 pounds, lightweight rowing has become the most competitive of all rowing events since its introduction. More than twenty-five countries regularly produce legitimate Olympic-contending boats. But despite its competitive appeal, only one lightweight event — the lightweight women's double — is contended at the Olympics. This in contrast to heavyweight rowing, which is contested in a number of different categories, with each country having the chance to enter upwards of seventeen women.

Nevertheless, Tracy was convinced of the rightness of her decision. She used the summer of 2004 to implement her weight-loss program and take a break from the sport prior to her four-year run to Beijing.

This was also the year of the Calgary Flames' run to the Stanley Cup. Fans across the city planned parties, crashed bars, and joined forces to cheer for their beloved team. And in the hockey-mad city that summer, Tracy met her own special Flames fan, Mark Duk.

Mark worked in Calgary's oil and gas industry and didn't know a thing about rowing. What he and Tracy shared, however, was an affinity for the outdoors. With Calgary as their base, the two used every opportunity they had that summer to go camping, hiking, and exploring in the Rocky Mountains. The two grew closer, and by the winter of 2004, they had made a commitment to see their relationship through the next four years.

~

From 1998 to 2006 they won nearly five times more Olympic medals than any other Canadian sport, and won more medals during this same time span than the sport had won during the previous eighty-two years. Even more astonishing is the fact that at the Torino Games in 2006 they equaled the medal haul (twelve) of the entire 2004 Canadian Olympic Team. Led by the three most dominant Canadian Olympic athletes of all time, they have combined to win 50 percent of Canada's medals at the past three Winter Olympics, thirty medals in total: nine in both Nagano and Salt Lake City, plus another twelve in Turin.

Who are they? Canada's speed skaters, arguably the most dominant group of Canadian athletes ever assembled in any one sport. Canada has become the predominant speed skating country in the world. When its skaters hit the ice, other skaters tremble.

Consider that since 1998 no country has won more Olympic medals in speed skating than Canada. Not bad for a country that thought it excelled only in hockey. In Torino in 2006, if Canadian speed skating was a country — the People's Democratic Republic of Speed Skating — its two gold, seven silver, and three bronze medals would have landed it ahead of both the host country Italy and Winter Olympic powerhouse Finland, for ninth place in the overall medals table.

Internal competition

Canada's speed skaters are tough on their opponents but even tougher on each other.

Winning the title of Speed Skater of the Year in Canada must be more difficult than solving world-wide climate change. Just ask Clara Hughes.

In 2002, Hughes became the first Canadian and only the fourth individual ever to win medals in both the Winter and Summer Olympics: She was a double bronze medallist in 1996 in cycling and bronze medallist in speed skating in 2002. Yet her teammates were busy scrambling to get Catriona LeMay Doan's photograph. LeMay Doan, the star of the speed skating team and Canada's flag bearer at the 2002 Games in Salt Lake City, became the first Canadian to defend a gold medal at any Olympic Games in the women's 500m.

In 2006, Hughes became the first woman in the history of the Olympics to win multiple medals in a Summer and Winter Games: Olympic gold and silver medals at the 2006 Winter Olympics to go with her two bronze medals in cycling from the 1996 Summer Olympics. Yet Canadians were intently watching their Olympic darling, Cindy Klassen, who skated to a Canadian record five medals at the 2006 Olympics.

Hughes' five Olympic medals aren't even enough to make her the most decorated athlete within her sport. That distinction goes to Klassen, whose six Olympic medals — five in Torino and one in Salt Lake City — make her the most decorated Canadian Olympic athlete of all time.

Hughes must be wondering what more she has to do to gain notice in Canada. She donates $10,000 of her own money to the Right to Play charity, a non-profit, volunteer organization committed to building playgrounds for underprivileged children around the world. Yet it is Klassen who is called "woman of the 2006 Olympic Games" by IOC President Jacques Rogue. It is Klassen whose wins the Lou Marsh trophy as Canada's top athlete in 2006. And it is Klassen who carries the Canadian flag in the closing ceremonies. Klassen, Klassen, Klassen. Hughes must think Klassen is the second coming of Wonder Woman.

Then there is Marc Gagnon.

Winning five Olympic medals in short track speed skating — three of them gold — Gagnon shared the distinction of being Canada's most decorated Canadian athlete in Olympic history with track and field athlete Phil Edwards. Until Wonder Woman came along, that is.

Then there are the sport's lesser accomplished athletes, whose successes would be almost folklore in any other Canadian sport. However, these athletes are considered just some of the many stars Canada has to offer in speed skating. For example, Jeremy Wotherspoon, a silver medallist at the 1998 Olympic Games and a legend throughout most of Europe, is the Wayne Gretzky of the sport. He's the winner of fifty-eight world cup races (as of March 2009), more than any skater in history, but most Canadians wouldn't recognize him if he was speed skating down the Rideau Canal. Naked.

Speed skaters Anouk Leblanc-Boucher and François-Louis Tremblay both won two Olympic medals in Torino and even their coaches forget their names. They're too busy watching Klassen.

Eric Bedard won four Olympic medals, two of which were gold, from 1998 to 2006, and all Canadians want to know is whether he has ever met Cindy Klassen.

Canada's speed skaters are so good that seemingly the only ones able to beat them are Canadians themselves.

Susan Auch beat every individual outside Canada at the 1998 Winter Olympics in the women's 500m. Unfortunately, she had to race a Canadian in Nagano — LeMay Doan — and had to settle for silver.

The same thing happened to Kristina Groves in 2006. She beat everyone except that Klassen girl.

The good news for all these individuals is that if they are named Canada's Speed Skater of the Year, there is a pretty good chance they'll also be Canada's Athlete of the Year.

The Bobbie Rosenfeld Award, given annually to Canada's female athlete of the year, might as well be renamed the Golden Blade Award. Four of the last eight recipients were speed skaters. If not for the fact that the Summer Olympics are held in an offsetting biennial from the Winter Games, Canada's speed skaters would probably win the award every year. Lori-Ann Muenzer won the award with a single gold medal at the 2004 Summer Games (she won it in cycling). Meanwhile, four Canadian women won multiple medals in the sport of speed skating at the 2006 Olympic Games and three of them barely got a handshake.

Two of the past seven recipients of the Lou Marsh Trophy, given annually to Canada's top athlete, have been speed skaters. If not for a couple of Canadians named Nash and Crosby, arguably the most dominant players of their generation in the sports of basketball and hockey, respectively, that number could be even higher.

The frightening thing is that Canada's speed skaters are only getting better. So good that Jay Morrison didn't even make the team that represented Canada at the 2007 world all-around championships in Heerenveen, the Netherlands, in spite of winning the 500m and finishing third in the 1500m at a world cup qualifier.

Kristina Groves and Jeremy Wotherspoon were crowned World Champions in 2008. Later that same year, at a world cup stop in Nagano, three Canadian women (Kristina Groves, Christine Nesbitt, and Shannon Rempel) finished in the top five in the woman's 1000m. Canadian development team skater Philippe Riopel set a new national junior record in the men's 500m race at a speed skating competition in 2007 and was later crowned world junior champion in the same event a few months later. In December 2008 Jessica Gregg, daughter of retired Edmonton Oilers defenceman Randy Gregg, picked up her second world cup medal in short track speed skating. And that Klassen girl is returning to the ice rested and ready to take on the world in Vancouver.

All of which leaves us to question *why* Canada's speed skating program is enjoying such unprecedented success.

The making of a juggernaut

Canada' success in speed skating began at the 1976 Olympics in Innsbruck, Austria. There, a seventeen-year-old Canadian named Gaetan Boucher first attracted international attention with a sixth-place performance in the men's 1000m. Boucher would be the sport's spokesperson within Canada for the next eight years, adding double gold and a bronze from the 1984 Olympics to his bronze-medal win from the 1980 Games in Lake Placid. With Boucher's success at the 1984 Games, the sport became popular with a new generation of skaters and participation increased as a result. In addition to his star power, the 1988 Games in Calgary saw the creation of North America's first indoor speed skating oval, which sparked additional interest in the sport, especially in Western Canada.

Increased participation was not translating into improved performances, however. Quite the opposite, in fact: Speed skating was struggling, and the results from the 1988, 1992, and 1994 Olympic Games showed it.

Armed with arguably the greatest speed skating oval in the world, the Olympic Oval in Calgary, Canada was failing to win medals in long track speed skating. Its best performance at the 1992 Games in Albertville was a seventh-place finish by Guy Thibault. At the 1994 Games in Lillehammer, Norway, Susan Auch ended a ten-year medal drought by winning silver in the 500m.

It was Canada's first Olympic medal in the sport since Boucher's gold in 1984.

Things were a little better in short track speed skating. Canada won three medals at both the 1992 and 1994 Games. However, the jury was still out on whether Canadian athletes could maintain their success. Short track speed skating was a newly introduced sport in 1992, and no one knew whether the initial success was by chance or by design.

"Up to the 1990s, Speed Skating Canada was a kitchen-table organization," says Jean Dupre, Director General of Speed Skating Canada. "We weren't sophisticated. There wasn't a lot of money and there was a lot of infighting among the board members themselves. It wasn't a good situation to be in."

In addition, the Olympic Oval wasn't being used as intended after the 1988 Games. "It was starting to be recognized as a white elephant. There were talks of converting it into a soccer field," says former Olympic speed skater Jacques Thibault. In 1992, however, Cathy Priestner Allinger, then the general manager of the Oval and Olympic medallist at the 1976 Games in speed skating, decided to kick-start things. She brought in Jacques Thibault himself to implement programs within the facility.

A winning mindset

Thibault was unique to Canadian sport in that he wanted Canadians not only to win on the world stage but also to dominate the sports landscape. As Thibault himself acknowledges, up to the early 1990s, this mindset didn't exist in Canadian amateur sport. "In Canadian sport, no one ever really dominated before ... There was the odd first or second place, but you didn't have a first, second, and fourth place performances in one event." Thibault's mindset from the very start was to change this way of thinking by providing athletes "with the opportunity to compete in order to be successful."

In pursuit of a dominant program, Thibault sought out the best speed skating coaches from all corners of the globe with the idea of making the Olympic Oval program the best in the world. As opposed to having just one coach with Speed Skating Canada, the Olympic Oval hired several, "a team of people who worked together for the benefit of the athlete," as Thibault puts it.

With a stable of world-renowned coaches in place, Thibault was able to retain his pedigree of coaches over a period of time through the Oval's association with the University of Calgary. Over 50 percent of the Oval's operating budget is provided by the U of C (the other 50 percent is provided by WinSport Canada). As a result, employees of the Oval have what employees in corporations across Canada expect to have. Employed through the university, they have a pension and are on a pay grid. They are unionized and offered a harassment policy. As a result of its association with the university, the Oval provides speed skating coaches with a compensation package that other Canadian sports can only dream of offering.

In addition to putting together a stable of professional coaches, Thibault encouraged international athletes to train at the Oval with the idea that the "best breed the best," as he puts it. "We were always nice and accommodating." In exchange, Canada's young athletes were seeing the world's elite performers on a daily basis.

With a team of world-renowned coaches, top-level international athletes, and well-funded support programs, the Olympic Oval began to look good in comparison with Speed Skating Canada. "National team athletes wanted to be a part of the Olympic Oval program," says Mark Greenwald, then director of the Olympic Oval. In 1994, recognizing the impact of the Olympic Oval on speed skating, the board of directors of Speed Skating Canada voted that the Oval program take over the national team program. Shortly thereafter, Speed Skating Canada became a client of the Oval. The latter hired the coaches, and Speed Skating Canada not only leased the ice within the facility but also agreed to use Oval coaches, thereby creating an integrated program. This isn't to say the two don't have their differences. However, they understand that they have the same goals.

The Oval understood that there were newer, better facilities in the world, and that they couldn't rely on past success to help withstand the changing needs of the sport. In keeping with its focus on attracting international talent, it was determined to have the fastest ice in the world. Thibault travelled the world studying humidity, air pressure, depth of blades, and so on, with the intent of attracting top-level athletes. The upshot was a long track ice surface that yielded, in 2006, an incredible seventeen Olympians, ten Olympic medallists, and sixteen Olympic medals.

Raising the bar for skaters

The Oval's desire to attract international stars may be a detriment to Canada's medal haul in the sport. Shani Davis of the United States sought the help of the Olympic Oval and its team of coaches in the lead-up to his gold-medal performance in the 1000m in Torino. But as Mark Greenwald of the Oval notes, "We look for (international) athletes where we are weak, with the idea of producing Canadian medallists in the future."

Speed Skating Canada, in contrast, is not interested in the development of international skaters. It has implemented initiatives that focus solely on assisting Canada's team. In the late 1990s, it developed a national training centre in the heartland of short-track speed skating, Montreal, Quebec. Armed with their own group of top-level coaches, Quebec athletes now can train without having to leave home.

Following the 2002 Olympics, in an effort to stay ahead of its competition, Speed Skating Canada sought the help of an Australian, Emery Holmik. Holmik had no prior experience within speed skating and was then the high-performance manager of Australia Volleyball. But as Jean Dupre, the Director General of Speed Skating Canada, explains, "At the time we didn't need a speed skating specialist; we needed a high-performance specialist to implement new strategies."

Dupre realized that hiring someone from outside the sport wasn't conventional, but it did turn out to be the right decision to move the organization forward. Holmik had an extensive background in strategic planning, management, partnership, development of high-performance programs, and experience with a variety of elite sports in the Australian sport system: precisely the qualities that Speed Skating Canada needed. The result was the implementation of high-performance structures that played a key role in Canada's success in 2006.

"Emery raised the bar for the long track program by giving us his expertise from the Australian high-performance sport system," says Gregg

Planert, the chairman of the Canadian high-performance committee for long track.

Holmik has since returned to his homeland to work at the high-performance centre in Canberra, but that hasn't stopped Speed Skating Canada from adapting to its environment and preparing for the 2010 Games in Vancouver. "Following Holmik's departure, we spent three weeks going through the delivery of our high-performance program," explains Dupre. This resulted in some tough decisions.

For example, Guy Thibault, head coach of Canada's powerful short track speed skating team, was let go. In his place, a new position, director of sport, was created, forging a closer link between high-performance sport and sport development. Two separate directors replaced the departing Holmik to oversee the high-performance programs in Calgary and Montreal. And international reinforcements were brought in to protect Canada's position as the world's dominant speed skating nation.

Finn Halvorsen, the Scotty Bowman of speed skating coaches, led the United States speed skating program to its best ever effort in Salt Lake City. In the hopes that he could duplicate this performance in Canada, Halvorsen was hired to oversee the country's long track program for the 2010 Games, working exclusively with Canada's athletes, through Speed Skating Canada.

However, in March 2009, when reports surfaced that there was dissension within the team, Halvorsen and Speed Skating Canada parted ways — this despite a number of medal-winning performances throughout his tenure. But don't think Speed Skating Canada has looked back. "We don't believe in doing the status quo — doing what we do every year," Dupre said. "We question ourselves and review everything and try to ensure that we are providing the athletes with the best possible environment and coaching."

With the athletes' concerns front and centre, Speed Skating Canada hired Dutch speed skating coach Ingrid Paul and United States sprint coach Michael Crowe. Paul helped guide Catriona LeMay Doan to Olympic Gold in 2002. Respected the world over, Paul also coached Dutch speed skating phenomenons Jan Bos to Olympic silver in 2002 and Bob de Jong to Olympic Gold in 2006. Crowe, meanwhile, was the U.S coach of the year in 1998 and 2002 and was instrumental in resurrecting the career of Jeremy Wotherspoon in 2007–2008.

The Koreans were developing skaters in short track speed skating who were faster than speeding bullets. Something had to be done in Canada, and fast. "We used to be the powerhouse in short track, but we've been passed," said Brian Rahill, Speed Skating Canada's director of sport, in an interview with the *Toronto Sun*. "They seem to have a little bigger engine than us and a sixth gear that we haven't progressed to yet." So, in an if-you-can't-beat-'em-join-'em scenario, Speed Skating Canada hired Korean coach Jae Su Chun for its short track skaters.

Chun left Speed Skating Canada in 2007 to work with the United States program, but his impact is still being felt. Canada's short track speed skaters credit him with turning their technique around and helping Canada catch up to the Koreans.

Despite the unfortunate loss of Chun, the following are just some of the staff that are presently employed through either the Olympic Oval or Speed Skating Canada:

- Xiuli Wang, a former world champion herself and winner of the Jack Donahue award as Canada's coach of the year in 2006. Clara Hughes calls Wang not only her coach, but also her mentor, one she would swim across the ocean to train with.
- Martin Gagne, Speed Skating Canada's male coach of the year in 2005.
- Derrick Campbell, team leader and coach on the U.S. Olympic team in 2006. (Upon hearing the news of Campbell's departure from the U.S. program, American speed skating star Apolo Anton Ohno called the loss of his coach "sad," and thanked him personally for "two great years.")

With the assembly of this coaching dream team and a sport executive that rivals that of the New York Yankees, expectations are understandably high heading into the 2010 Olympics. Speed Skating Canada, with the assistance of the Olympic Oval, has targeted sixteen medals in Vancouver, or nearly one medal for each event contested. (There are twenty events contested in short and long track speed skating at the Olympics.) Meanwhile, Canada's *entire field* of summer athletes won eighteen medals at the 2008 Olympics.

5

Icing on the Cake: Canada's Recipe for Success in Vancouver 2010

In 2005, with the arrival of spring, Tracy's feet were firmly planted in Victoria. The weight was coming off nicely. She had transformed herself into the most powerful lightweight rower in Canada.

Tracy's home away from home during the four-year buildup to Beijing was Rowing Canada's boathouse on Elk Lake. A five-minute drive from Victoria, Elk Lake had that cottage feel that many Canadians have come to enjoy during the summer months. With a lack of local amenities nearby, it is a nature wonderland for Victoria residents breaking free of the daily grind. Hundred-year-old forests dominate the landscape to the east and north. On the banks of the southernmost section of the lake, near the highway, is the boathouse.

The two-storey structure would have looked like an abandoned greenhouse if not for the multitude of cars parked nearby. With its lack of suitable offices for coaches and its run-down athletes' lounge, complete with worn carpet and torn couches, the facility gave little indication that it was home to Canada's best rowers. The change rooms — right down to the wooden benches — resembled the moldy dressing rooms found in old Canadian skating rinks. The showers were littered with empty shampoo bottles, and the toilets gave off the stench of week-old urine.

It was a far cry from the high-performance facilities that Tracy had expected. But that didn't matter to her. She was making an impression on her coaches. In the two months since taking up residence in Victoria, she had progressed from being the third- or fourth-fastest lightweight in camp to being a contender for the top spot on a weekly basis. Her body was slowly adjusting to becoming a lightweight, and her coaches were already planning their world championship crews around her.

In addition, Tracy was now engaged to be married to Mark, who had proved to be a quick study in the sport of rowing. "Men without cox," "woman with cox," " stroke rates," and "boat run" were becoming part of his everyday vocabulary. He also understood the financial challenges that Tracy faced and began developing unique ways to finance her rowing career.

Tracy was still not carded in 2005, despite training at Rowing Canada's training centre in Victoria. Up to that year, she was still an unknown in lightweight rowing, and as a heavyweight rower in both 2003 and 2004 she hadn't shown the potential to receive money as part of Sport Canada's Athlete Assistance Program. However, with the help of his friends in the oil patch, Mark started organizing poker tournaments in Calgary. Half of the proceeds from these tournaments went to finance Tracy's training, with the other half going to the victor. It wasn't much, but Tracy appreciated everything she received. Mark's friends enjoyed having the opportunity to help an aspiring Olympian while at the same time enjoying an evening with friends. It was a win-win.

The support of friends like those in Calgary made Tracy reflect on how fortunate she was. She was in pursuit of a dream, doing what she loved, and in an environment dedicated to excellence. And above all, she felt joy in knowing that there was a group of friends back home who recognized her efforts and supported her in her dream.

Tracy was on cloud nine in Victoria. But then, in May 2005, she was asked to move to London, Ontario.

Canada has the unenviable record of being the only host nation of two separate Olympiads — the Summer Olympics in Montreal in 1976, and the Winter Olympics in Calgary some twelve years later — to fail to win an Olympic gold medal on home soil. To avoid achieving this dubious distinction a third time, John Furlong, CEO of the Vancouver 2010 Olympic Games, made it known that the only way the Vancouver Games could be considered successful was if Canadian athletes won medals. He went on to add that, for this to occur, "Sport needs a chiropractic adjustment. We have never had an attitude for winning in this country. We have to adjust this. We have to create a culture of winning, where not only do we say we want to be the best, but we believe we are the best. A belief where not only our athletes believe, but the public and media feel it as well."

Own the Podium

This feeling of being the best has been building in winter sport since the Calgary Games in 1988. In 2004, with the Vancouver Games a mere six years away, the COC, the Vancouver Organizing Committee for the 2010 Games (VANOC), Sport Canada, CODA (now WinSport Canada), and the thirteen winter sport federations collaborated in making Canada the number-one sporting nation in the world. A radical proposition for a country that had never finished higher than third in medals at the Olympic Games.

Late in 2004, Cathy Priestner Allinger, an Olympic silver medallist in the sport of speed skating at the 1976 Olympics, and an independent task force of winter sport specialists from around the world were brought together. Their purpose was to formulate a plan for how Canada would achieve this lofty goal.

Priestner Allinger and her team of international sport experts spent several months interviewing each of the collective winter sport organizations. They also looked at what the world's top performers had in terms of equipment, research, and "performance enhancement teams" of massage therapists, technicians, and sport psychologists. Their findings: Canada's winter sport organizations didn't have the services necessary for success. "Almost 100 percent of our winter sports in Canada had less," Priestner Allinger said in an interview with *Maclean's*. To bring Canadian athletes on par with its competitors, the task force recommended an additional $110 million in sport funding and a change in attitude toward winning.

The task force anticipated that Canada could achieve its goal in Vancouver through targeted funding, the implementation of a top-secret program (which involved enhanced technology, research and development, and human-performance research) and the introduction of a high-performance commission. This five-year plan, called Own the Podium (OTP), was designed to put Canada's top athletes on the podium by giving them the resources they needed to win.

This being a plan that the sport organizations themselves believed in, sport officials set about putting it into action. "We said to the sports, we'll get you the money," noted Chris Rudge, chief executive officer of the Canadian Olympic Committee (COC), in an interview with The Fan 590. They realized that they had to "stop going to the government begging for money," he said. He and the COC accordingly sought and found half of the $110 million from corporate sponsors through VANOC before approaching the government for the other half. In March 2005 the federal government responded by promising to fund the remaining $55 million. (Note that OTP funding has since increased to $120 million, with the extra $10 million coming from the Canadian Olympic and Paralympic Committee.)

With the funds to carry out the plan, sport officials then went to work with the creation of a high-performance commission.

In December 2005, Dr. Roger Jackson, Olympic gold medallist in the sport of rowing, former dean of kinesiology at the University of Calgary, former president of the Canadian Olympic Committee, and highly respected sport official, was anointed CEO of the Own the Podium program. Jackson was responsible to develop and implement the recommendations of the OTP report, as well as to issue recommendations regarding the most effective ways to allocate resources.

A few months later, Canada's winter athletes went to Torino and had their best Games ever.

Following the Games themselves, bravado was everywhere. "We hit the targets we established," said Chris Rudge, chief executive officer of the Canadian

Olympic Committee, referring to the OTP's goal of twenty-five medals and a top-three finish. "What is more important is we knew why we did it."

Sport officials boasted that the success in Torino was largely attributed to the OTP program. According to Olympic officials, the OTP plan ensured Canadian athletes in Torino had access to a larger support staff of nutritionists, sport psychologists, massage therapists, and medical staff, which made all the difference. "The depth of the athletes and the support they have right now are greater than they've ever been," said Cathy Priestner Allinger, who wrote the OTP report.

Added Alex Gardiner, then director of coaching and international performance for the COC, "It's clear that several of our high-performance initiatives have had a direct and positive effect on Canada's athletes."

Undoubtedly so, but one has to wonder if the OTP program had the effect Canadians initially were led to believe it would. After all, even Chris Rudge, CEO of the COC, acknowledged prior to the Games in Torino, "it takes many years to move an athlete from midrange to elite." One has to wonder, then, about the significance of the OTP program without the initiatives of WinSport Canada and sport organizations like Speed Skating Canada. After all, Canada's Olympic heroes were already proving themselves on the international scene years prior to the OTP's implementation.

For example, Cindy Klassen, the winner of five medals in the sport of Speed Skating at the 2006 Games, was a bronze medallist at the 2002 Games and in 2003 was the first Canadian in twenty-seven years to win the all-around title at the World Speed Skating Championships.

Pierre Lueders, a silver medallist at the 2006 Games in the two-man bobsleigh, won the gold medal in the very same event at the 1998 Olympics in Nagano, six years prior to the introduction of the OTP report.

Clara Hughes won two medals in the sport of long track speed skating in Torino. And while she acknowledges that the OTP program gave her the opportunity to be the best she could be in Torino, her first Olympic medal came at the 1996 Olympic Games, nearly eight years prior to the program's introduction.

Duff Gibson, the 2006 Olympic gold medallist in the sport of skeleton, won the world championship in that sport in 2004, months before its introduction.

Bob Storey, president of the International Bobsleigh and Toboggan Federation, feels that Canadians won't know the effects of OTP until the 2014 Winter Games at the earliest.

However, as Ken Read, CEO of Alpine Canada, noted, OTP is "the icing on the cake" for Canadian athletes, over and above the core funding of their sports by Sport Canada. He added that OTP can be an important finishing touch that puts a good athlete over the top. Proof of this can be found in the positive effect the program has had on Canada's skeleton team. The program paid for the cost of testing sleds and suits in an Ottawa wind tunnel at a cost of $15,000 an hour. The return on this investment? Canadians won three medals in the sport in Torino.

The bobsleigh teams were able to review video of their performance between training runs. Canada's curling teams were sent to Norway in September 2005 to gain valuable international experience.

The extra funding from the program allowed freestyle skier Jennifer Heil to have personal coach Murray Cluff with her at the Games. Heil won gold.

Canada's women's hockey team could afford the $850 cost of an MRI examination in a private clinic and start rehabbing knee injuries more quickly than if they had to wait for the procedure in a public hospital. Canada's women's hockey team won gold.

As the COC's Chris Rudge said of the OTP program, "One of the things that's really positive is we know the athletes are going into competitions focused on the right things, not on backfilling issues regarding a place to stay or being able to afford travel."

With the Torino Games now a distant memory and all Canada's focus on the Winter Games in Vancouver, Canada still has some work to do to achieve its goal of becoming the top winter sport country in the world. After all, we finished third in the overall medal count in Torino, behind Germany and the United States. But with thirteen fourth-place finishes and 132 Olympic rookies having gained experience on the team in Torino, there is strong sentiment that our athletes can achieve their goal. With WinSport Canada providing the facilities, sport organizations like Speed Skating Canada and the Olympic Oval producing the athletes, and OTP providing the necessary financial resources, there is little doubt that Canada is on the right track ... in winter sports.

PART TWO

Why We Lose at the Summer Olympics

6

The Truth Revealed: The Sorry State of Our Summer Efforts

Every woman rower training with Canada's national centre in Victoria packed her bags each April and moved to London, Ontario — only to move back to Victoria in November. Tracy was no different. London was home to the women's national rowing team. Team sponsors were there, and so was the team's head coach, Al Morrow.

With the winter thaw now complete in eastern Canada, Tracy was packing her bags, cleaning her apartment, and preparing to leave for London the next day. The national training centre on Fanshawe Lake was opening for another year, and Canada's women rowers were expected to report there by April 15.

Tracy was moving for the second time in less than five months. This meant booking and paying for an airline ticket and finding a new apartment in an unfamiliar town.

Like Elk Lake in Victoria, Fanshawe was an outdoor playground, in its case for residents of Southern Ontario. The t-shaped lake came complete with a golf course on one shore and a campground on the other. But for Tracy this was no playground: It was a battleground.

Canada's lightweight group was bursting at the seams with the return of athletes from colleges and universities across the continent. Tracy found herself in a dogfight. There were only two available seats, and as many as ten women showed themselves capable of taking a seat on any given day.

Day in and day out she battled for a spot. By late spring, a trend was emerging: Tracy was one of the fastest doubles rowers in camp. With the arrival of summer, it was apparent that her time had come. She was chosen to represent Canada in the lightweight women's double at a world cup race in Lucerne, Switzerland.

$\sim$

"It isn't a fair comparison," barks Ron Bowker, a Canadian track and field coach at the 1988 Olympic Games. "In athletics you are competing against over two hundred countries, (but) in speed skating they have maybe twenty competitive countries."

"You can't compare winter and summer sports," says Daniel Igali, Olympic gold medallist at the 2000 Olympics. "One quarter of the world competes in the Winter Games. At the Summer Games there are two hundred plus countries."

The arguments are virtually the same throughout Canada's summer sport movement. In an attempt to defend their performance at the Olympics relative to their winter counterparts, Canada's sporting authorities are quick to note the competitive imbalance that our summer athletes face. And on first glance, they should.

Only thirty-nine of the International Olympic Committee's 203 countries have ever won a Winter Games medal. No winter medals have ever gone to a country from Latin America, Africa, Southeast Asia, or the Middle East. There is little argument that the Winter Olympics are dominated by about fifteen northern countries wealthy enough to afford the high-cost facilities and equipment necessary for all of the winter events.

However, when one pulls back the veil just a little, it becomes clear that the competitive pool isn't as deep as summer officials would like to believe.

Rowing, canoeing, gymnastics, trampoline, cycling, diving, fencing, weight-lifting, sailing, shooting, equestrian, archery, and, to a lesser extent, aquatics are all capital-intensive sports, and the number of medal-winning countries within these sports is virtually as limited as it is in winter sports.

Only forty-two countries have ever won an Olympic medal in rowing. No nation from the Middle East or Southeast Asia and only one African nation, South Africa, can lay claim to a medal-winning performance in the sport. In diving and archery, only twenty countries have ever won medals; in gymnastics it is thirty-six countries. Middle East and African nations have never medalled in any of these sports. Fewer than fifty nations have ever won medals in aquatics. Furthermore, the results from the past three Olympiads show that no country from the Middle East or Southeast Asia, and only three from Africa, have won medals in the pool. And this sport is considered largely universal.

And despite the edge that Canada should therefore have in these summer sports, our athletes aren't dominating these activities the way we are speed skating, hockey, and virtually every other winter sport.

Not only are our summer sporting organizations not winning, but our summer sporting organizations are struggling. This phenomenon is especially evident when Olympic events with high rates of participation by Canadians are examined.

Consider that between 1988 and 1996, Canada won a total of thirteen Olympic medals, four of which were gold, in the sports of track and field and swimming. At the past three Olympiads, Canada's swimmers and track and field athletes laid claim to a combined three bronze medals. Canadian cyclists won six Olympic medals at two Olympiads in the 1990s. Since the turn of the century, however, Canada's cyclists have had two medal-winning performances, at the past three Olympiads. Canada's boxing program was ranked among the top ten in the world from the late 1980s to the mid-1990s. How times have changed. Our boxers haven't won an Olympic medal since 1996, and Boxing Canada is now ranked in the bottom 10 percent of the world.

Many of our programs are not even qualifying for the Olympics. Canada qualified only three teams (softball, baseball, and women's water polo) out of a possible fourteen for the 2004 Games. In traditional team sports that are played by millions of Canadians each day, such as basketball, soccer, and volleyball, Canada failed to qualify a single men's or women's team.

Canada did qualify five teams (men's water polo, men's field hockey, softball, baseball, and women's soccer) for the 2008 Olympic Games, but noticeably absent were our basketball and volleyball teams. The 2008 Olympiad was the third straight in which Canada's men's and women's volleyball teams didn't participate. In basketball, Canada's men's and women's teams both failed to qualify for the second straight Olympiad, marking this country's longest ever absence from the Olympic tournament in this sport. The men's basketball team even failed to qualify for the 2006 world championship, for the first time in over forty years.

Daniel Igali, an Olympic gold medallist at the 2000 Olympics in wrestling, agrees that Canada is not doing very well in summer sports, noting that "Cuba is a third of the size of Canada, and wins nearly twice as many medals as we do."

Culture or choice?

All of which leaves Canadians to question why Canada's summer sporting organizations are doing so poorly. Igali says that the reason we do well in sports like speed skating and falter at the Summer Games is that there is a skating culture here in Canada. As he explains, "Parents want to teach their kids to skate. They don't teach them to box or wrestle."

Trevino Betty, a high-ranking sport official with the Commonwealth Games Association in Canada, supports this argument. "Canadians have a psychological advantage on the ice that we don't have in summer sports."

However, as little as fifteen years ago, Canadians were more successful in the sports of rowing, swimming, and boxing than in long track speed skating. And athletics, not speed skating, was considered Canada's most prolific Olympic sport.

As Canada's speed skaters were struggling to find the mark in the 1990s, Canada's summer athletes were enjoying unprecedented success. At the 1996 Summer Olympics, Canada won a record twenty-two medals. Among them were medal-winning performances in track and field, cycling, boxing, men's wrestling, volleyball, and canoeing. The 1996 Olympic Games proved that Canadians could compete in sports that mattered to Canadians (as evident in participation rates published by Sport Canada).

And then things dried up almost overnight.

What happened?

Graham Hood was a Canadian Olympian in track and field at both the 1992 and 1996 Games. He agrees with the argument that the Summer Games are significantly more competitive than the Winter Games. However, he feels that Canada's lack of performance at recent Summer Olympiads has more to do with decisions made by the sports organizations themselves than with a stronger competitive field. Decisions made at that level, he says, "are made to protect positions, rather than think outside of the box." He adds that within his own sport of athletics, many of Canada's best athletes are produced outside the country, himself included.

Perdita Felicien, Canada's best hurdler and an Olympic medal favourite at the 2004 Olympics before falling on the first hurdle in the Olympic final, trained with U.S. coach Gary Winckler in Champagne, Illinois.

Mark Boswell, a two-time medallist at the world championships in the high jump, trained in Austin, Texas, with his coach Dan Pfaff. The latter also coached Canadian Olympic gold medallists Donovan Bailey, Glenroy Gilbert, and Bruny Surin at the 1996 Olympics.

Pfaff, interestingly, has produced more Canadian Olympic medallists over the past fifteen years than Athletics Canada's team of coaches. Meanwhile, Martin Goulet, who coached athletics in Canada for fourteen years before being promoted to the position of chief high-performance officer for the organization, hasn't coached a single medallist at either the (Senior) World Track and Field Championships or the Olympic Games.

Nevertheless, when it comes time for the Olympic Games, Goulet's name seems to be one that is always called. Having coached at the 1992, 1996, 2000, 2004, and 2008 Olympics, Goulet has become a Canadian fixture when Canada's track and field teams compete internationally.

A system of ineptitude

Hood and Donovan Bailey contend that Athletics Canada perpetuates a system of "ineptitude" when it fails to reward the coaches who are producing winning athletes.

Unfortunately, the situation at that organization pales in comparison with problems in many of Canada's summer sporting organizations.

Russ Anber, a boxing analyst with TSN and the CBC, notes, for example, that "Boxing Canada is presently a mess, and does about half of the things it needs to do."

This is something that isn't lost on Pat Fiacco, an official with Boxing Canada and the mayor of Regina. He claims there is a serious lack of leadership within Boxing Canada. "The current administration is dysfunctional at best," he says. "There isn't a permanent national coach, there is no national training centre, our funding has been reduced, and we have half the membership we used to have." He also notes that boxing is run by an "old boys club," citing as an example the hiring of the president of one of the provincial associations to manage a national team.

All of which may explain why boxing, once one of Canada's prolific sports, hasn't produced an Olympic medallist in twelve years, failed to win a single gold medal at the 2006 Commonwealth Games for the first time in its history, and qualified a single athlete — Adam Trupish — to the 2008 Olympic team. Not surprisingly, Trupish was knocked out in his opening match at the 2008 Games.

Similar headaches present themselves in the Canadian Soccer Association (CSA). In 2006, Colin Linford took up the role of president of the CSA, determined that the organization be more like a business than a "kitchen-table organization run by volunteers." In May 2007 he hired Fred Nykamp, then the CEO of Basketball Canada, to be CEO of the CSA. However, Linford resigned in August of that year when the organization failed to ratify Nykamp's hiring. For his part, Nykamp sued the CSA for wrongful hiring and firing, and the two parties settled for an undisclosed amount.

With all of these ongoing problems, it's little wonder that the on-field performance of Canada's national soccer teams has suffered as well. The women failed to advance past the first round of the women's world cup in 2007, prompting harsh words from national team coach Even Pellerud over what he sees as a lack of support for his program. At the 2007 U-20 World Cup, hosted on Canadian soil, the men's team failed to score a single goal. The senior men's program hasn't qualified for an Olympic Games or world cup since 1986. And if that was not enough, the women's soccer team, considered a contender for a medal in the 2008 Olympic Games, finished a disappointing eighth, losing in the quarterfinals to the United States.

How badly off is Basketball Canada? As Michael Grange, a reporter with the *Globe and Mail*, puts it, "Basketball Canada makes the Canadian Soccer Association look like Donald Trump." Consider that disgruntled executive Fred Nykamp had jumped at the chance to leave Basketball Canada for the Canadian Soccer Association.

Those within the sport of cycling have been known to light up online chat rooms across the country, and for good reason. Employees in the sport's governing body are jumping ship faster than passengers on the Titanic. Road races that were fixtures across the country are now inexplicably absent in Ontario, Alberta, and Manitoba.

World-class athletes like three-time Olympic medallist Curt Harnett and Olympic gold medallist Lori-Ann Muenzer, who once were fixtures of the Canadian landscape, are now inexplicably absent, as demonstrated by the sport's lacklustre performance in Beijing. And the individual overseeing everything was Lorraine Lafrenière, the sport's CEO, who admitted that she knew little about the sport she led.

Prior to working with Cycling Canada, Lafrenière was employed in varying roles within Canada's sports community, but never as a sports executive in a national sport organization. The result? Under her watch, Cycling Canada's Olympic medal count dropped from two in 2004 to zero in 2008. However, the blame does not rest solely with Lafrenière, who resigned in March 2009. Since 2004, the sport has had no fewer than four different CEOs at its helm.

But it would be foolhardy to think that problems within cycling, boxing, basketball, and soccer stop at the executive level. Soccer, boxing, and now basketball are all reeling from financial problems. These three sports were all facing financial deficits in 2008. Things have gotten so bad in basketball that, according to a CBC report, in 2008 the organization was charging national team athletes to attend training camps. Word on the street has it that cycling is bleeding money. Even rowing, a sport that enjoyed unprecedented success in Beijing, winning four Olympic medals, found itself in the red in 2008.

Then there is swimming. Alumni, sponsors, parents, and athletes of the Canadian swim team flooded Canadian newspapers with messages during the Summer Games in Athens in 2004 saying that the sport had to get its act together. Swimming Canada dismissed coach Dave Johnson after the Games, in September. Johnson managed the swim program for more than a decade prior to that. During his tenure, the medal count of this program fell from three Olympic medals at the 1996 Games to one in 2000 to none in 2004.

Membership plummeted while controversies abounded.

In 2000, Johnson hired twenty-six-year-old coach Shauna Nolden to assist him at the Sydney Games. The Canadian Swimming Coaches Association objected, saying that Swimming Canada had failed to select the female coach on the predetermined criterion of having an athlete on the Olympic swim team. An appeals panel agreed. However, rather than abide by the decision, Swimming Canada changed its own selection criteria to tailor the posting to Nolden's credentials.

At the 2002 Commonwealth Games, Canadian swimmers failed to win a single gold medal, the first time this had happened since 1958. And Johnson stirred up controversy during those Games by chastising Jennifer Carroll, a Quebec athlete, for waving the fleur-de-lys flag. The issue created such a stir that Sport Canada threatened to revoke Swim Canada's annual funding of $1.78 million. Johnson was known to deflect blame for his program's non performance on his own athletes when they failed to deliver at major competitions. An independent report on the 2002 Commonwealth Games noted that the swimming athletes were demoralized, divided, frustrated, and angry, and that Canadian athletes in other sports sensed the poisonous atmosphere around the squad.

In 2004, athletes berated the press, the press berated the athletes, athletes sued the organization, and everything imploded before Swimming Canada finally decided it was time for a change. And while Canada's swimming team showed a dramatic improvement at the 2008 Olympics in winning a bronze medal — Ryan Cochrane in the 1500m freestyle — there is little doubt that the mismanagement of four years earlier continues to haunt the program.

The frightening thing is that athletics, boxing, cycling, basketball, and swimming are some of Canada's best-run summer sporting programs. In fencing, athletes have to organize their own flights and hotels for competitions. Catherine Dunnette, an Olympian in women's épée at the 2004 Games, notes that fencing hasn't had a coach since those Games, with hardly any coaches coming up the ranks to fill the void. Today, with no coach, it is extremely difficult for developing athletes to make the team. As Dunnette says, "International competitions count toward your national ranking, but only the top three or four people get their flights paid for. Everyone else has to pay for their own, creating a system where the team that represents Canada at international competitions is defaulted to the team that went to the Olympics." Today Canada's épée team has little funding and no sponsorship funding.

Sherraine Schalm, the star of Canada's fencing team and Canada's first-ever medallist in the sport, at the 2005 world championships, trains on her own in Hungary, a decision she credits for getting her to where she is in her career. Unfortunately, shortly before the start of the 2008 Olympics, Schalm was told by her coach that she was no longer welcome to train with the Hungarian national team. She lost in the opening round of the Games to a Hungarian.

Things aren't much better in sailing, where Olympian Martha Henderson has to organize her own car rental and hotel in preparation for international competitions in Europe. Henderson finished thirteenth at the 2008 Games in Women's Yngling-Keelboat.

In beach volleyball, athletes have to pay for their own volleyballs and coaching, while also organizing their own travel schedules. Conrad Leinemann, a two-time Olympian in the sport, feels that funding for beach volleyball has been reduced in order to put money into Volleyball Canada. It's no surprise that Canada failed to qualify a men's or women's beach volleyball team for the 2008 Olympic Games.

Balkanized boards

Despite the myriad of problems that persist in Canada's summer sport organizations, little can be done if the sports involved choose to do nothing. In Canadian amateur sport today, fifty-two sport federations make up the board of directors of the coc, but the sports themselves are accountable only to their own board of directors, many of whom have little idea of what is transpiring in their programs.

The directors of Rowing Canada are not unlike those of any other sporting organization in Canada. They are volunteers who try to balance full-time jobs with family. Fortunately for Canada's rowers, they are extremely devoted to their sport and this is exemplified in the sport's success at recent Olympiads. However, not all sports are so fortunate. Many boards are composed of individuals who don't have the time or commitment to make an educated evaluation of the national team program. This in turn creates a complex situation where the directors of the national sport organizations accept the recommendations of those they employ with little or no consequence should things falter. And those the sport organizations serve — like the coc — can only sit and watch. Chris Rudge of the coc agrees, saying that the coc is like the "ham in the middle of the sandwich" between national sport federations and the sport-funding arm of the Canadian government.

Bob Storey, president of the International Bobsleigh and Toboggan Federation, feels that the sport organizations in Canada, for the most part, are not responsible. He notes that "successful sports in Canada create their own success."

Randy Starkman, a writer with the *Toronto Star*, agrees. "In Canada, if a national sport organization is faltering, there is no mechanism for someone to step in and do something."

Sport Canada, the funding arm of the Canadian government, has the ability to revoke funding to sport organizations. But that doesn't mean it is prepared to get involved in running a sporting organization if deemed necessary.

Fortunately for winter sport organizations, there is a mechanism through the leadership of WinSport Canada that makes them accountable. Because these organizations rely on the facilities in Calgary, and WinSport is determined to see the facilities used for the development of high-performing athletes, the association has no qualms about helping an organization restructure itself for the benefit of the athletes.

With its focus on the development and maintenance of world-class facilities, WinSport does not like to get involved in the day-to-day activities of sport organizations. But it will intervene if the need arises. Bill France, WinSport's vice president, sport, says, "There was a time when the sport of luge was losing money, had limited coaching, and was poorly organized. CODA (WinSport) stepped in and helped with talent identification, provided financial assistance, and offered office space at cost. It is now a better-run group."

A similar situation arose in ski jumping. In 2004, with the assistance of WinSport in hiring accredited coaches, Canadian ski jumpers competed at the 2006 Olympics for the first time in over ten years.

And don't forget speed skating. WinSport provides 50 percent of the operational budget for the Olympic Oval, which is largely responsible for making speed skating the medal-winning juggernaut it is today.

While WinSport's mandate is to preserve the Winter Olympic facilities from the 1988 Olympics, what success summer athletes have attained over the past two Olympiads can be attributed in part to ... WinSport. Carol Huynh, a wrestler and gold medallist at the 2008 Olympic Games, trained at University of Calgary facilities developed in part by WinSport.

Kyle Shewfelt was the beneficiary four years earlier, winning gold in the sport of gymnastics. A graduate of WinSport's National Sport School, Shewfelt trained at WinSport's own Calgary Gymnastics Centre, a facility heralded as a cross-training dream for winter sports. If only all summer sports were appropriate cross-training activities for winter sports. Then maybe WinSport could provide leadership for the entire Canadian sports community.

7

Purchasing the Podium: Canada's Plans for Improving Olympic Results

Lucerne is to rowing what Broadway is to the stage. The Swiss city's Rotsee is known simply as "the lake of the gods," and it is the perfect venue for a rowing race.

The finger-shaped lake is protected on both sides of its 2400-metre shoreline by thick forest foliage and a series of gentle hills. A nature reserve for much of the year, the Rotsee opens its waters once a year to the international rowing community as the traditional venue for the final leg of the rowing world cup series. The Rotsee is the Yankee Stadium of rowing and in 2005 Tracy had the privilege of enjoying her first international rowing race there.

She was welcomed by two Swiss soldiers holding automatic machine guns guarding the entrance to the athletes' compound. Flashing the accreditation that she had received a few hours earlier, Tracy walked into a world that many only dream of.

There before her, all within earshot of each other, were athletes of every national stripe: Russians, Americans, Cubans, English, French, Italians, and Germans, Chinese, and Japanese. Forty-one countries were represented, all of whose representatives appeared to speak a different language. For Tracy, the place was a peaceful amalgamation of every culture of the world.

And everywhere she turned were the superstars, including Ekatrina Karsten of Bulgaria, the three-time world champion in the women's single, and Olaf Tufte, the defending Olympic gold medallist in the men's single from Norway. It was intimidating for Tracy, but she was grateful for the chance to meet and compete against the world's finest in her sport.

Experience, not winning, was the goal Tracy and her coaches set for this her first international regatta. Not so for her doubles partner Liz Urbach, who had competed at the non-Olympic world championships, a regatta for boats that are not eligible to compete at the Olympics. (Events that aren't contested at the Olympics are contested at a non-Olympic world championship in an Olympic year. Urbach competed in a light-weight women's quad — a non-Olympic event — in 2004.)

Drawing upon her international experience, Liz helped guide Tracy to a sixth-place result. Not bad for their first regatta together as a double and Tracy's first international rowing regatta on the world's most famous rowing course.

The twosome returned home to Canada more determined than ever. The potential for success at the upcoming world championships in Japan was high. All they needed was time to gel.

Rowing Canada, meanwhile, had different plans. Canada's most accomplished lightweight rower at the time — Mara Jones, an Olympian at the 2004 Games — was returning to Canada's lightweight program. After only a few weeks back in camp, it was clear to Canada's coaching staff that its sixth-place lightweight double needed a shake-up. Tracy's partner was out and Mara was in.

It takes time to row in perfect unity with another rower. A world-class boat requires that its two occupants have time to get to know each other's idiosyncrasies and make adjustments. With only a few weeks left before the start of the world championships, the two scrambled to work things out. They knew that with proper coaching, success was possible.

However, before they even had a chance to get to know each other, they were moving yet again. Tracy was heading back to Victoria, marking her third such move in a little over seven months. This one, however, was for a short time. Rowing Canada had made it known that athletes intending to compete at the upcoming world championships in Japan had to first time-trial their boats in Victoria. Tracy and her partner were not to be excused. The results from the time trial would decide who would be on Canada's national rowing team at the 2005 world championships.

～

Heading into both the Summer and Winter Games in 2004 and 2006, respectively, Canadian athletes were supported as never before. The ratio of support staff to athletes was higher than it had ever been at any previous Olympiad: more than one to one, which according to many would translate into medal success.

Moments before the 2004 Games in Athens, Chris Rudge stated, "The coc is committed to supporting excellence, and our mission is to ensure Canada's high-performing athletes have the necessary resources to achieve podium success at the Olympic Games."

Similar sentiments were expressed by Canada's winter athletes heading into Torino. "I've been an athlete at this level for fifteen years in two different sports and with all the changes I've never seen it this good," speed skater Clara Hughes said in an interview with the *Calgary Sun*. "I feel like my coaches have all the support they need, and as an athlete all the little things that were causing a lot of stress have been addressed."

The results at both the Athens and Torino Games told a distinctively different story: Canada's winter athletes won; Canada's summer athletes did not.

Dr. Roger Jackson, ceo of the Own the Podium program, noted that the results in Torino were "very significant in terms of demonstrating Canadian support for high-performance sport. With Canada's strong showing at the recent Olympic and Paralympic Winter Games in Torino, and the increased financial and technical support provided to winter sports, we are well on our way to achieving the goals of the Own the Podium 2010 initiative."

Without a $110-million program of its own, Canada's summer sport program failed miserably in Athens, leading some to believe that Canada's summer sport failures were caused by lack of funding. But Mark Lowry, then the executive director of the COC, begged to differ, saying, "Those results (twelve medals in Athens) weren't about money."

So why is it, then, that Canada's sporting brass requested an additional $510 million to revamp its amateur sporting program following the Athens Games?

A cry for help

There were cries for help, and for change, on every hand following the debacle in Athens. "We have to change the sports system," said Chris Rudge, CEO of the COC. "We have to change what we are doing. We have to be more about excellence."

"The rest of the world is leaving us behind ... The model we have in this country doesn't work," said Lowry.

A few months later, Canadians were introduced to the Own the Podium program, a radically new type of initiative that sought to place Canada in the top three of the medals at the 2006 Winter Olympics and on the medal podium in 2010 more often than had ever been accomplished before. A short year later, Canada's winter sporting body achieved the first of its goals in Torino. Witnessing the success of their winter counterparts, Canada's summer athletes soon began to ask, "What about us?"

Road to Excellence

In response, Canada sporting brass started developing a program, for Canada's summer athletes, similar to Own the Podium (OTP). As the COC's Mark Lowry noted, "We believe that Canada's summer athletes deserve the same chance to succeed as those who compete in winter sports."

The business plan, called Road to Excellence (RTE), was presented to the Canadian public for the first time in June 2006. Upon initial review it appeared to be a duplication of the winter plan. Following the pattern of the

OTP plan, the RTE envisioned that Canada could achieve a top-sixteen finish at the 2008 Summer Games and a top-twelve finish by 2012, through targeted funding, innovative research (enhanced technology, research and development, and human-performance research), and the creation of a multi-organizational committee leading to the development of a coordinated sport system. And the author of the report, Dr. Roger Jackson, was the CEO of the OTP program.

Based on the merits of the OTP program, Canadians were led to believe that the RTE program was all that Canada's summer athletes needed to achieve Olympic success. And who would dare argue? After all, OTP had catapulted Canada's winter athletes to Olympic glory.

"With the initial success of the Own the Podium 2010 initiative, I am confident in the sport community's ability to develop and execute a similar initiative to help Canada's summer athletes and coaches reach the podium," said the COC's Chris Rudge. "The Road to Excellence business plan provides a blueprint for how we can provide Canadian summer sport athletes with the essential tools and resources necessary to achieve success."

Fast out of the gates

The OTP program had been greeted by the Canadian public with scepticism, given its lofty expectations of a number-one finish in 2010. The RTE plan, in contrast, was met with anticipation, and this quickly turned to outright excitement with the hiring of Alex Baumann. On September 24, 2006, in a crowded ballroom in downtown Toronto, Baumann was anointed as the saviour of Canada's summer sporting system with the announcement that he had been appointed executive director of the RTE program.

Baumann was an Olympic gold medallist at the 1984 Games in Los Angeles in the sport of swimming, and winner of the Lionel Conacher award as Canada's male athlete of the year — that very same year. He knew what it would take to revamp Canada's summer sport system. After all, he had served as executive director of the prestigious Queensland Academy of Sport in Australia, which had produced many of the country's top Olympic athletes.

"I believe I can have an impact," Baumann said on that inaugural day. "I'm under no illusions about how difficult this job will be. It might mean two steps forward and one step back, but I'm looking forward to the challenge."

Some eighteen months later, Canadians were still waiting for Baumann and the RTE plan to take that initial step.

At the heart of the RTE program was a request for an additional $510 million to help implement the recommendations of the report. But by February 2008, a mere five months before the commencement of the Beijing Games, a measly $10 million of that amount had been raised.

And with time ticking down to the commencement of the Beijing Games, the COC turned its frustration on the one organization it had promised it would stop begging for money, the federal government.

"One hopes we might someday get political support for amateur sport in this country, but it's clear it's not there yet," Rudge said. "In the time this government (Conservatives) has been in office, they've done virtually nothing for making an investment in high-performance sport." And in an interview with the Sun media network, he said, "We find ourselves in a situation akin to saying to one child, we really support your dreams and hard work and aspirations and saying to their sibling, I'm sorry, but you don't get anything. It grates with your sense for fair play."

Criticism, however, turned to optimism in March 2008, when the federal government approved funding of $72 million over a four-year period to help Canada's summer athletes prepare for the 2012 Games in London.

Rudge responded to this by saying, "This investment is the culmination of a long, collaborative process between the sport community and the government, and I want to congratulate Secretary of State Helena Guergis for her timely leadership on this file. With this funding, the Road to Excellence Program will be able to take a big leap forward in putting programs in place to help Canadian summer athletes reach the podium at upcoming Olympic Games."

But will it? COC officials readily admitted that the funds did little to prepare our athletes for Beijing, "We wish we had the money one year ago, but we're still working for 2012 and beyond," said Sylvie Bernier, the Beijing chef de mission, who won a gold medal in diving at the Olympic Games in 1984.

Prior to the start of the Beijing Games, even Baumann himself questioned the impact of the RTE program in its first two years of operation. "I don't expect a lot of gains (in the Beijing medal count) but I'm hoping we can do better than Athens. Ultimately, the 2012 Games is where we need to see a shift."

Let's not forget, however, that the RTE program, as first presented to the Canadian public, recommended $510 million to help support Canada's summer athletes. From 2008 to 2012, the RTE program is due to receive $72 million in government funding: $8 million for 2008-2009, $16 million for 2009-2010, and $48 million for the two years leading into the London Games. And now Canada's summer athletes are told they may have to share these monies with their winter counterparts. This is hardly the support necessary to carry out the initiatives of the RTE report.

Then again, finances were one area the authors of the RTE report failed to consider fully, whereas they were front and centre in the OTP plan.

In January 2005, the Vancouver Organizing Committee for the 2010 Games (VANOC) purchased the COC's Olympic marketing rights until 2012 to help finance the high cost of staging the 2010 Games. Recognizing the importance of having winning athletes on the podium in hosting a successful Winter Olympics in 2010, VANOC agreed to provide OTP with 50 percent of its requested $110 million dollar budget from its Winter Olympic sponsorship agreements. With half of the required $110 million in place, the federal government agreed to provide the remaining $55 million.

Unfortunately, the performance of Canada's summer athletes at the 2012 London Games has little bearing on VANOC and its desire to host a successful Winter Games. As a result, the RTE plan can't rely on Olympic sponsorship agreements for funding. Rudge suggested the RTE could look to philanthropic donations and other sources for revenue. But in the end, one indisputable fact remained. The RTE plan sought nearly 85 percent of its $510-million budget from government sources (provincial and federal), almost forgetting that, according to Canadian sport policy, a blueprint for sport in Canada, regional (provincial) governments were supposed to be removed from high-performance sport altogether.

With the provincial and federal governments showing no interest in footing the full $510-million price tag on its own and no one willing to provide a secondary source of funding, the RTE has had to downsize on several occasions. The program began in 2006 with a requested $88 million per year in funding. This was later, in 2007, reduced to $30 million per annum. The program will now have to settle for a paltry $8 million in 2008-2009 before a continued source of funding arrives. And even then, funding will be capped at $24 million per annum unless funding from alternative sources can be found.

But even if every penny of the requested $510 million were made available to the RTE, would the program achieve its desired results? COC officials point to the success of the OTP program as evidence it could. "I'm very optimistic about the future of Canadian summer sport after seeing the Road to Excellence Business Plan," said Iain Brambell, a COC official and three-time Olympian in rowing. "We've seen the success Canada's Winter Olympians and Paralympians had in Turin and certainly this program has the potential to help summer athletes reach the podium in both 2008 and 2012."

But make no mistake, the RTE plan is not the equivalent of its winter counterpart. The OTP report, presented to the Canadian public shortly after the 2004 Athens Olympics, was written with input from international sport experts the world over. In formulating the report, Cathy Priestner Allinger sought the advice of international sport experts such as Herwig Demschar, who helped guide famed U.S skier Picabo Street to Olympic Gold in 1998. She also looked for advice from the likes of Jacques Thibault, general manager of the Olympic Oval in Calgary, who was instrumental in revamping Canada's speed skating program.

Meanwhile, the RTE plan sought the advice of Alan Roaf from the sport of rowing and Charles Parkinson from volleyball. In 2006, Roaf was squeezed out of Rowing Canada after the organization restructured its high-performance program, while Parkinson served as volunteer team committee chair for a sport that hasn't had a team (indoor) compete at the Olympic Games since 1996.

The remaining portion of that answer can be explained by examining the state of winter and summer sport in Canada.

There *is* an I in team

The RTE report, like its winter counterpart, recommended that sport funding be prioritized based on a sport's potential medal success, a radical proposition in Canada for a sporting system that was widely perceived as egalitarian. But the OTP plan also looked at the sport's importance in Canadian culture.

Not so with its summer equivalent. The RTE program prioritized sport funding solely on a sport's medal potential at upcoming Olympiads. This explains in part why niche sports that are enjoyed by few Canadians — trampoline, diving, and rowing, for example — brought home the lion's share of medals in Beijing: They received a disproportionate share of sport funding. Meanwhile, common everyday activities that are at the heart of Canadian sport — soccer, boxing, badminton, volleyball, basketball, and field hockey — suffered the consequences.

When news struck that rowing coach Bent Jensen had been diagnosed with pancreatic cancer, the COC approved the last-minute addition of an extra coach, Howie Campbell, to help him with his duties in Beijing. Meanwhile, the COC denied boxer Adam Trupish's request to have the customary two corner men, which most boxers enjoy, in his corner in Beijing.

In preparation for Beijing, the RTE program helped fund physio, massage, the services of a sport psychologist, and medical treatments for both trapolinist Karen Cockburn and diver Alex Despatie. In contrast Anna Rice, a badminton player, sold Team Canada clothing and equipment to Canadian badminton fans at local competitions to raise much-needed funds for her travels.

And if times are tough on the likes of Rice, the RTE program has all but forgotten about team sports that are part of the Olympic program. In January 2008, Volleyball Canada was forced to pull out of the sixteen-nation World Volleyball league because the RTE program revoked $500,000 in sport funding earmarked for the organization.

Roger Jackson defends the move, noting that team sports such as volleyball can produce at best only two Olympic medals, while individual sports like rowing can produce a plethora of medals. "It was this sort of methodology that guided East Germany's sporting system to prominence in the 1980s," he says.

However, the thinking behind this process doesn't sit well with Adham Sharara, president of the International Table Tennis Federation. Sharara says that RTE-type programs are "narrow-minded." He notes that under this program, a youngster who is seven feet tall and a magician with a basketball would have no chance of becoming an Olympic athlete. "All sports are subjected to highs and lows over time," he adds. "If Canada focuses its efforts on only those sports that produce medallists at upcoming Olympics, over time Canada will be left with a system that funds two or three sports. This would negatively impact our status as a sporting nation." Sharara compares it with how a wise country with a shortage of engineers or doctors makes sure that it doesn't reduce funding to those professions.

Such comments are not lost on Andy McInnis, a track and field coach and high-ranking track official in Canada. "Podium is the new catchword. I hear it from all the sport bureaucrats. If you're not on the podium, you're not any good. If you can't convince us that you have the potential to be on the podium, then you're not any good. What are Canadians doing painting a picture like that? I don't understand. It's caused by tying funding to success. We are restricting funding, getting less and less, and it's a big toilet bowl. It's spinning and slowly going down."

Olympic gold medallist Daniel Igali acknowledges that winning is important, but adds that sport funding can't focus on high performance alone. "It is not only the top line that scores in hockey."

All of this explains why the Own the Podium plan works. Under that plan for winter sports, capital-intensive sports like ski jumping and skeleton suffer at the hands of more popular team activities like hockey despite the fact that in an "absolute best case scenario," hockey can produce, at best, two Olympic medals at any given Olympiad. In Torino, Canadian athletes won three medals in skeleton and only one medal in hockey.

Under OTP, funding is geared toward hockey as opposed to other medal-rich sports because "everything spins off hockey," says Trevino Betty, a former athlete himself in track and field, and director with the Commonwealth Games Association of Canada. "Kids build rinks in their backyards from coast to coast across Canada." Cindy Klassen is a hockey player turned speed skater. World champion figure skater Kurt Browning started out as a hockey player, as did Duff Gibson, Olympic gold medallist in the sport of skeleton. World Champion Jeremy Wotherspoon started speed skating as a way to prepare for an upcoming hockey season. Olympic medallist Jeffrey Buttle, a figure skater, started skating on hockey skates. Ditto for speed skater Clara Hughes. The list goes on and on.

If only the same were true of summer sports.

In 2004, according to a study by Sport Canada, the sports of ice hockey, skating, skiing, and curling, all high-priority sports under OTP, also had the highest levels of participation. Meanwhile, the most popular summer sports by participation (volleyball, basketball, tennis, badminton, and soccer) were prioritized near the bottom of the funding ladder under RTE. In that program, capital-intensive sports like rowing, which report participation rates of less than 0.1 percent of the Canadian population and require expenditures of tens of thousands of dollars to pay for boats, were classified as high priority, receiving the lion's share of funding. Today Rowing Canada receives more sport funding than track and field, basketball, volleyball, badminton, boxing, and every other summer sport organization in between. Is it plausible to think that everything will spin off rowing in the near future? Canada's sporting bureaucrats seem to think so.

A flawed approach

Following on the heels of the policy of tiering sport funding based on a sport's likelihood of success, the RTE report argued that if Canada increased sport funding by $510 million from 2006 to 2012, the country could finish in the top twelve of the medal count in London 2012. RTE figured that for Canada to achieve this, it would have to win approximately twenty-five medals, or one additional medal for every $39 million invested in sport ($510 million/ thirteen additional medals over and above the Athens medal count). Without the additional funding, Canada could expect to maintain the status quo of twelve to fourteen medals at a Summer Olympic Games (twelve being the number achieved in Athens).

In comparison, the Own the Podium program introduced in 2005 sought to inject an additional $110 million per annum into sport. Sport experts argued that with the additional funding, Canada could win an additional eighteen medals (over and above the Salt Lake City medal count of seventeen) by 2010, or one additional medal for every $6.1 million invested ($110 million/eighteen additional medals).

Sport experts argued that the additional investment under RTE was required because there were more than two times the number of sports to service. Dr. Dan Mason, a sports management professor in the faculty of physical education and recreation at the University of Alberta, has a problem with that assumption. "We see other countries that are more successful, but I think it's more important to mimic their delivery system rather than expecting x number of dollars to equal y number of medals."

This comment isn't lost on Alex Baumann, executive director of RTE. "My feeling is that right now we have an imbalance in terms of where the resources are going, particularly on the summer side," he said in an interview with the *Toronto Star*. "That's why we don't have the resources going into coaching and programs." And while he sees potential, he notes that a coordinated, integrated sports system doesn't exist in Canada on the summer side. He adds that it's working splendidly for winter sports in places like Calgary, which he calls "a kind of a high-performance precinct."

There is little doubt that things have improved for Canada's summer athletes since Baumann took control. However, under the terms of RTE, should they be allowed to continue improving? Even Baumann recognizes that "there is no egalitarianism in high-performance sport," going on to say, "We can't be all things to all people."

Therein lies the rub.

Think about it. With a summer sport program that failed to meet its goals in 2004, winning a lowly twelve medals; with a summer sport program that failed to beat Belarus in the medal count in Beijing; with a summer sport plan that plans to win one additional medal for every $39 million invested into sport, it is clear that Canada's summer sport program is not as performance oriented as its winter counterpart. Consider that our women won sixteen of Canada's twenty-four medals at the 2006 Winter Olympics. Furthermore, a number of Canadian women narrowly missed the podium in Torino. Among those fourth-place finishers, skier Kelly VanderBeek came the closest, missing out by three hundredths of a second. Under Canada's new-found performance-based system, shouldn't most of Canada's high-performance dollars be invested in winter sport programs that cater solely to women?

Dr. Roger Jackson, CEO of Own the Podium, notes that "women's sport is less competitive then men's sport, and as a result isn't a fair comparison." Fair or not, Jackson himself, as author of the RTE report, did not consider the "competitive strength of a sport" as a factor in prioritizing sport funding; in fact, just the opposite.

Ian Reade, who wrote his thesis on sport funding, confirms that under the RTE plan, Canada appears to be going after the "low-hanging fruit." Reade says that the goal of RTE is to win medals, so sport officials are giving a lot of opportunities to less-competitive sports to meet that goal.

Jackson defends the move; however, this notion that Canada has to put money where it has the best opportunity for success creates a Catch-22. Canada's Olympic officials defend targeted funding, but they seemingly fail to comprehend that under a targeted funding structure, the RTE plan shouldn't exist.

Walt Macnee, a director with the Canadian Athletes Now Fund, feels that under the RTE program, the COC wants to have their cake and eat it, too. "The Olympic Games are a business and the COC manages that business in Canada," he says. "As a business enterprise here in Canada, the COC can't afford to have half of its business enterprise critiqued every four years at the Summer Olympics."

Ian Reade agrees. "Summer sports are high profile here in Canada, and the Canadian government cannot afford to look anaemic when it comes to these sports ... Something has to be done."

Money isn't everything

But should the RTE plan be the blueprint for the future?

Kevin Wamsley, an Olympic historian with the International Centre for Olympic Studies, says no — that medals aren't something "you can predict with a business plan." Wamsley is not alone in his beliefs. Reade, coaching concentration co-ordinator with the University of Alberta's faculty of physical education and recreation, whose Ph.D. thesis focuses on this question, says, "I don't see any possible negative aspects to putting more money into sport, but there is no evidence to suggest that it will translate to more medals. Of course money is going to help, but does it lead directly to medals? I think there are more factors at play."

Reade's research includes comparing government funding among sports from 2000 to 2001, four years before the Athens Olympics. The team that received the largest pool of money ($1.8 million) was swimming, and that team failed badly at the 2000 and 2004 Games.

Marvin Washington, a professor at the University of Alberta, acknowledges that while the RTE program, and, to a lesser extent, the OTP program are wonderful policy statements, they aren't really effective, because they are, in essence, run by government. "Both programs look to government to provide the funds and as a result aren't so much strategic programs but rather political programs trying to satisfy the broader constitutional base," he says. He asks us to imagine a scenario in which a program said it wasn't going to fund wheelchair sports because they were underperforming on the international stage "There would be political fallout from the decision. Political decisions minimize the effectiveness of the overall program."

Jackson, CEO of OTP, disagrees, noting that both OTP and RTE are both independent of government and, as a result, are accountable to their funding partners.

However, when asked who's in charge of the RTE plan, Reade of the University of Alberta is quick to point out that "he who has the gold makes the rules." The federal government is the single largest financial contributor to both programs. "With the recent sponsorship scandal, the biggest goal for Sport Canada (the sport-funding arm of the federal government) is accountability," he says. "For every one dollar spent, eight dollars are spent to make sure it is spent appropriately. Under the RTE and OTP plans, Sport Canada has become an accountability agency whereby the COC is telling Sport Canada how to spend the money and the federal government watches it." He concludes by saying that under both sport plans, "The COC wants to make all the decisions and the federal government has bought into it. Sport Canada is playing nice because, should things falter, (the federal government) wants to say that it wasn't their fault."

All of which prompts Washington to say that the problem with a government-controlled high-performance system is that there is no accountability — that it's too political and not strategic enough. History tends to support the argument. Look at the progression of events: Canada falters in Athens. The sports involved deflect blame onto the government for a lack of resources, with virtually no sport or sporting organization willing to accept accountability for its failures. Political pressure mounts across Canada, from citizens and sport organizations alike. Then, with the Vancouver 2010 Olympics in Canada's own backyard, and the country never having won a gold medal on home soil, the federal government gives winter sport the resources and the money it needs.

Meanwhile, without the political push of their winter cousins and without a high-profile event in Canada anytime soon, summer sport programs sit and beg for every dollar they can find.

8

Who's Driving the Bus?
The Leadership Problem

In the fall of 2005, Rowing Canada's plan was to send two lightweight boats to the world championships in Gifu, Japan.

As opposed to the Olympic Games, where the only event for lightweight women was the double, the lightweight quad event was also contested at the world championship. Recognizing the importance of the Olympic Games, however, most countries placed little importance on this non-Olympic event and had their best athletes competing in the double.

Despite having to travel across the country, having little experience together, and having little time to acclimatize themselves to Canada's west coast, Tracy and Mara were confident that the results from the time trial would show everyone that they could race with the world's best on the international stage. Most observers would have agreed that this lightweight double was a lock to qualify. Meanwhile, Canada's lightweight quad had an outside chance of qualifying. But that is why Rowing Canada time trials its boats prior to a major championship: to determine which boats truly are fast.

According to the results of the time trial, Tracy and Mara were not as fast as first expected. Meanwhile, the quad, consisting of four lesser athletes, exceeded expectations. In the opinion of those overseeing the time trial, the quad had the potential to medal in Japan, while the double would have a difficult time making the final. It was clear. Rowing Canada would send a quad to the world championships, and not a double.

The situation presented a further dilemma. Should Rowing Canada send a lightweight quad that deserved to be there, leaving its two best lightweight athletes in Canada, or take two deserving athletes out of the quad and give their seats to Tracy and Mara?

In the end, Rowing Canada chose athleticism. Tracy and Mara were going to Japan, while two athletes from the quad were told to go home. The decision was harsh, but with only twenty-four hours till departure to a pre-world championship camp in Japan, no one had time to complain. Tracy later would admit to feeling guilty about the decision.

Regardless, she was packing her bags to row at the world championships with a crew she had never been with before.

∾

In the Academy-Award-nominated song "Blame Canada," from the movie *South Park*, Canada is blamed for the downtrodden state of American society. The lyrics start in with, "Times have changed. Our kids are getting worse. They won't obey their parents. They just want to fart and curse! Should we blame the government? Or blame society? Or should we blame the images on TV? No, blame Canada! Blame Canada!"

Coaches, athletes, officials, and experts alike are all in agreement regarding whom to blame for the state of summer sport in our country. The refrain of their song is, "Blame the Canadian government!"

Following Canada's non-performance at the 2004 Olympic Games, whom did the COC blame? The Canadian government. Michael Chambers, president of the COC, said Canada's poor showing was the result of government cutbacks.

"The current low level of government support will not achieve the Olympic results Canadians desire and our athletes deserve."

Amateur athletes struggle to make ends meet. Blame the federal government. "Canadian Olympic hopefuls are reduced to the level of the homeless, standing on street corners with their tin cups," said IOC member Paul Henderson. He laid the blame for Canada's problems in amateur sport at the feet of Paul Martin, who was finance minister in 1996 when, according to Henderson, sport funding was slashed to about 5 percent of what is spent in France and the United Kingdom.

Is the criticism justified?

Sport Canada

Canadian amateur sport is managed through the federal government as a division of the International and Intergovernmental Affairs sector called Sport Canada, within the federal department of Canadian Heritage. Its mission is to enhance opportunities for Canadians to participate and excel in sport.

Despite its importance, Sport Canada seems to be an afterthought of the federal government. Over the last seven years, the government has appointed eight different individuals to lead it and the individual overseeing matters at the 2008 Olympics wasn't a minister but rather a subordinate to a minister within Canadian Heritage — the difference being that a subordinate can't introduce government bills. And the individual appointed to the role was Helena Guergis, whom acclaimed political columnist Don Martin called "a lost cause ... and over her head."

When all is said and done, it is little wonder that the leadership of Sport Canada has been called into question. "We need leadership from the top," says Chris Rudge of the COC. "Someone's got to say that sport is important. I've seen three ministers responsible for sport, none of whom had any power or mandate to effect change."

Even Stephen Owen, the former minister of sport, seemed to agree with this statement. Moments before the Athens Olympics began in 2004, he noted that he does not make sport policy but only "reflects it."

It is Canada's amateur athletes, of course, who often take the fall for the government's actions. In December 2005, hockey player Shane Doan got into a quarrel with NHL linesman Michel Cormier when Cormier supposedly overheard him say, "F—ing French," in response to a disputed call. The NHL looked into the matter and felt there wasn't a problem. Doan was exonerated, but that didn't prevent a Liberal MP and once minister of sport, Denis Coderre, from lashing out at Hockey Canada's decision to select Doan for the 2006 Olympic team. "If he doesn't make the appropriate apologies for his anti-francophone and intolerant statements, he should be expelled from the team," Coderre said in a letter to Hockey Canada president Bob Nicholson. "Mr. Doan has not only insulted our country's francophones, but the vast majority of Canadians."

Despite statements made by both the NHL and Doan proclaiming his innocence, Coderre persisted in his efforts to have Doan disciplined. In January 2006, Doan filed a lawsuit against Coderre for defamation, seeking $250,000 in damages and promising to contribute to charity any damages awarded to him. In April 2007, Coderre filed a countersuit, seeking $45,000 in damages. And then the real bandstanding began.

In May 2007, after Doan was named captain of Team Canada for the forthcoming world championships, all four political parties voted to have Hockey Canada directors appear before a House of Commons committee to explain their actions. Don Cherry called the action ridiculous. Canadians flooded radio talk shows expressing their dismay at the government. Through it all, Doan was the epitome of class, carrying Canada's world championship team to gold. His teammates and coaches didn't hold back from weighing in on the government's decision.

"That whole thing was a joke from the beginning," said defenceman Eric Brewer in an interview with TSN. "It was a total waste of time and people should have had better things to do than care about that."

Coach Andy Murray echoed the sentiments. "He was a tremendous leader for us all the way through. I'm not much of a politician. I'm more of a hockey coach. When I see stuff like that, I just shake my head."

Unfortunately it isn't uncommon to see amateur sport suffer because those who manage it seemingly forget its importance in Canadian society.

When asked about the dual portfolio he had assumed in late 2006 as minister of intergovernmental affairs and minister of sport, Peter Van Loan said, "I think (Intergovernmental Affairs) is a pretty good (portfolio) for anybody who cares about the country a great deal." He added that he had always been interested in the political side of politics, "and you have some sports thrown in for fun."

Some ten months later, with the departure of Van Loan and the appointment of Helena Guergis as Canada's head of sport, the delivery may have changed, but the message remained the same. In late 2007, George Gross of the *Toronto Sun* reported Guergis as saying that sport wasn't a priority of the Conservative government.

And when its leaders fail to recognize the importance of sport in Canada, sport becomes a platform to build up the pocketbooks of government loyalists.

"From 1998 to 2002, with help from Paul Martin's staff, a group of Montréal sport promoters received more than a million dollars in federal sponsorship grants, but only 'an infinitesimal portion of the money' ever reached the amateur sport organizations for which it was intended. Under the chairmanship of Martin's close political ally, Serge Savard, Internationaux du Sport de Montréal (ISM) — a non-profit amateur sport promotion company — tapped over $8 million in funding from various levels of government, but *repeatedly* 'failed to deliver the goods.'" This according to an eight-part exposé by the sport department of *Le Journal de Montreal*, and later reported on in a blog by Ian Gillespie.

Gillespie reports, "According to *Le Journal*, the placement of the Canada wordmark at a Montréal judo meet was used by ISM to justify $30,000 of its sponsorship grant for the year 2000. The judo organization in question, Judo-Québec, received only half that much from ISM. Patrick Esparbes, executive director of Judo-Québec, revealed to *Le Journal* that 'in 2001 and 2002, (they) did business directly with the federal government and ... received $25,000 a year; that's $10,000 more than the amount (they) were given by ISM.'

"In 2000, ISM also left its mark on the Air Canada Cup midget triple-A hockey championship. Again, according to *Le Journal*, ISM was given $20,000 in sponsorships to have the Canada wordmark hung at the tournament and included in the event's program. For its part, ISM was supposed to line up sponsors for the tournament itself but failed to do so. Subsequent to ISM's failure, other sponsors were eventually found; ironically, they were themselves government agencies (the Armed Forces and the RCMP).

"This raised questions as to what the $20,000 actually paid for. Event organizers did tell *Le Journal* that they were pleased with important logistical work done by personnel granted to them by ISM. However, these personnel had apparently already been paid from ISM's operating budget — a budget that had, in turn, already been paid for through grants from Economic Development Canada and the province of Québec."

The list of ridiculous spending goes on. ISM was paid $50,000 to profile great Canadian athletes in its quarterly magazine, a magazine with a circulation of just ten thousand copies. ISM was also paid to fly the Canadian flag in its own lobby.

And it doesn't end there. In 2004, FINA, the governing body for swimming, pulled the 2005 World Aquatic Championships from the city of Montreal because of a lack of corporate sponsorship. The event was later reinstated after the city's mayor, Gerald Tremblay, guaranteed financing any shortfall in the $60-million budget. But with ISM and Francis Fox — the former principal secretary to Prime Minister Martin and the head of ISM's predecessor, Montréal International — heavily linked to the event, questions remain regarding how the federal government's $16-million investment was spent.

Self-appointed leader

With a federal government unwilling to acknowledge the importance of sport in Canada, and with WinSport largely focused on Canada's winter sport program, the Canadian Olympic Committee is trying to fill the summer leadership void. The problem is that the COC is not an athletic organization but a marketer of the Olympic brand here in Canada.

First recognized by the International Olympic Committee in 1907, the COC is one of more than two hundred National Olympic Committees (NOCs) worldwide responsible for promoting the fundamental principles of the Olympics around the world.

As Canada's representative to the International Olympic Committee, the COC is also responsible for ensuring that Canada's athletes participate at the Olympics. The IOC states that only an NOC can send teams and competitors to participate in the Olympic Games.

Proudly promoting the Olympic ideal in Canada, the COC's importance has steadily grown over the last hundred years. As of March 2009, it had five offices across Canada and was made up of seventy-nine board members. Meanwhile, eleven board members head the United States Olympic Committee. The COC has become a sporting juggernaut seemingly accountable to no one, despite relying heavily on public funds. Are Canada's amateur athletes benefiting?

According to Randy Starkman of the *Toronto Star*, in the late 1990s the COC organized an Olympic lottery to help raise funds for Canada's amateur athletes. But instead, the lottery ended up losing $10 million of future athletes' money. Two of the principals behind the botched venture went on to take up good jobs with COC sponsors, and the CEO of the COC at the time, Carol Anne Letheren, emerged unscathed.

The 2004 Games were considered a failure by Canadians despite renewed optimism within the COC that it had turned the corner, pointing to an $8.7-million investment called The Excellence Fund. More than $7 million was dispersed, based on the recommendations of a technical support panel to assist athletes in their athletic pursuits in preparation for the 2004 Olympic Games. But according to the COC's own annual report, some of the recipients of the fund retired following the 2000 Olympic Games.

During the Games themselves, many of the athletes expressed frustration over the provision of services offered by the COC.

Nearly a third of Canada's athletes skipped the opening ceremonies in Athens, some with the hopes of getting some last-minute medical treatment prior to the start of their event. These athletes, however, would have to wait till the next day for that treatment — because Canada's support team was marching in the ceremonies.

David Ford, a world champion white water kayaker and three-time Olympian, wanted to travel to Athens on the same flight as his kayak. It had become a ritual for him since 1996, when his boat was crushed while being transported by air to the Atlanta Olympics. The coc had wanted to fly Ford's kayak to Athens five months prior to the start of the Games. Ford, however, needed to keep his kayak in Canada for his training. By the time the matter was resolved, Ford and his boat were booked on a later flight at a higher ticket price. He had to cover the difference in cost.

"It's frustrating for me," Ford said. "I'm very successful at World Championships and world cups when I'm able to run a program the way I want to. But that's not the way it is here. I suffer for that, come Olympic time." Ford finished fourth at the Athens Games.

Listen to Canada's amateur athletes and you'll learn that Ford's situation isn't that uncommon, leaving one to question whether the coc, whose main job, as mentioned, is promoting the Olympic brand, should be managing sport in Canada.

An Olympic battle

In 2005, Jane Roos found out the hard way just where the coc's efforts should, and shouldn't, lie.

In 1997, Roos, a former athlete in her own right, established the See You in Sydney fund, the sole purpose of which was to raise money for Canadian athletes. She came up with the idea while sitting on a hospital bed following a serious car accident. The fund started small. In that inaugural year, Roos managed to raise $50,000 for Canadian athletes by organizing Loonie and Toonie promotions at corporate offices across Toronto.

By 2000, however, Roos not only was collecting donations from ordinary Canadians, she also was garnering support from corporations. She was able to continue the fund past Sydney to See You in Salt Lake City and See You in Athens initiatives. In the process, the fund redistributed more than $4 million in private and corporate donations to Canadian athletes through individual grants of $6,000.

Since those early days, Roos and her fund have helped over five hundred athletes, winter and summer alike. Prominent Olympians like Daniel Igali and Adam van Koeverden benefited from the fund and have acknowledged that it was instrumental in their pursuit of Olympic Gold. "When no one else knew me, (Roos) provided me with money so I could pay my rent," Igali said. And van Koeverden added, "Being able to rely on that kind of cash flow to supplement my training that way comes in handy."

Of those who did medal in Athens, a common theme emerged time and time again: that they received the monies they required from the See You in Athens fund. Out of the twelve Canadian medallists in Athens, eleven were recipients of monies from the fund.

Through Roos, athletes were rising to prominence within Canada and corporate Canada was coming forward to assist with the cause.

In 2004, Molson Canada announced that it would donate $3 million to support Canadian athletes through Roos, while MasterCard agreed to give her $500,000. But these high-profile donations came at a price.

The media speculated that corporations were avoiding the high cost of Olympic sponsorship and riding the Olympic brand on the back of Roos.

In 2004, it was rumoured that Labatt Breweries walked away from its sponsorship of the Olympics Games in Athens because of Molson's announcement of support through Roos. Labatt denied the rumour, saying that the "Summer Olympics aren't as targeted to our audience as other properties. With respect to exclusivity, it's not something we need to have with all of our properties (and that includes) the Olympics."

Adding to the matter was the fact that VISA, an official IOC sponsor, invested $100 million U.S. to be affiliated with the Olympics. Meanwhile, MasterCard, VISA's rival, through a $500,000 donation to Roos and her fund, could say it was supporting Canada's team.

All of which made the COC angry, thinking that both Molson and Master-Card had sidestepped the COC's proper control over the Olympic brand. "I think that ethically, if you're looking for an association with Athens, you should be going through us," said Mike Patterson, the COC's director of marketing.

But as Walt Macnee, president of global markets for MasterCard, said, "MasterCard's intentions were pure. It was a non-political move. Here's the money, give it to the athletes. No rules were broken."

The COC disagreed, saying that the fund was making a thinly veiled allusion to the Games with the name of an Olympic city in the name of the fund.

Roos, however, says the COC knew of the association with the fund and chose not to do anything four years earlier. She says that in 2000 she hired the marketing company IDL&M, which at the time formally represented the COC, to check out what was then the See You in Sydney fund. IDL&M determined that there wasn't an association between the two non-profit firms. As a result, the COC seemed to accept Roos and her fund. But when Roos started to infringe on the COC's territory and started garnering huge corporate donations, things got nasty. According to Roos, a COC executive told her in 2003 that the COC was the Queen Mary and that she was a little tugboat. "We can take you out at any time," he said. The COC in turn, used its influence to sink not only the tugboat but also Canada's athletes.

In 2005, tired of having sponsors sidestep its high-priced marketing agreements, the COC took action. Following the Athens Games, the COC invoked its status as a government-recognized public authority, using its power under the Canadian Trade-marks Act to adopt the See You In ... trademark as its own. Roos' marketing efforts came to a sudden halt and more than $60,000 of the fund went to stage a legal battle to keep control of her organizations name, "money that should be going to the athletes," she said.

Olympic gold medallist Adam van Koeverden called the COC's actions crazy. "Why would you want to see something that's helping out so many people and doing nothing negative not go on? (The See You In ... fund) is a necessary part of the Canadian sports system."

"The COC can't attack its own athletes — it can't attack the Olympians," added gold medal rower Jake Wetzel.

The COC saw it otherwise, however. David Bedford, the organization's executive director for revenue generation, brand management, and communications, defended the move. "What we were doing was protecting the rights of companies who have invested in an Olympic association ... The move was entirely justified."

Justified, because back in 1983 the COC was granted public authority, implying that they could adopt someone else's trademark and use it as their own. However, in order to do so, the COC had to prove that they in fact used the See You In ... trademark in its own promotional materials. Something it could not do.

But before Roos could defend herself in a court of law and protect Canada's amateur athletes, she was forced to re-brand her organization under a new name, Canadian Athletes Now. Under Canadian law, the COC was entitled to absorb the original See You In ... brand until a legal challenge was issued.

Roos did challenge the issue and in April 2007 succeeded in winning back her name. The judge who presided over the case recognized that the COC had overstepped its boundaries in protecting its image. But Roos acknowledges that in the end, she lost. "We won in the court but no one really wins here because it has been distracting and such a waste of energy."

Meanwhile, the COC hasn't looked back, using the Olympic brand to impact all Canadians who play sport.

Lord of sport

In 2007, the COC received nearly $1.5 million in public funds. However, the money trail ends there for the Canadian public. As part of the federal review process, multi-sport organizations that receive federal sport monies are required to submit audited financial statements to the government. But the COC is the only major sport organization in Canada not bound by such requirements. In comparison, WinSport publishes audited financial statements and makes them available to all on its webpage.

And when an organization is seemingly unaccountable to those who fund it, the interests of the organization begin to manifest themselves.

There was a time when the Commonwealth Games, world championships, and world cups mattered to Canadians. Television coverage of the Commonwealth Games used to be round-the-clock for fourteen straight days. World championships used to be broadcast in prime time. Oh how times have changed.

Today, with the introduction of the Own the Podium and Road to Excellence programs, the COC has systematically altered amateur sport in this country. Under these programs, the focus of Canada's amateur sport system is on a two-week event hosted every two years. Meanwhile, every other international sporting event has virtually fallen off the amateur sport landscape.

Not a single Canadian metropolitan newspaper sent a journalist to report on the 2006 Commonwealth Games in Melbourne, Australia. Relying on news agencies, television coverage of the event was reduced to a one-hour highlight package late at night.

"There's a perceived hierarchy in Canada and of the importance of the different Games, and unfortunately, from a media and public standpoint, I don't think the Commonwealth Games have been given the profile they deserve," Ross Outerbridge, Canadian chef de mission, told Reuters.

In 2007, Gary Reed became the first Canadian since 1964 to win a medal in a distant event at a global championship when he won silver in the 800m at the World Track and Field Championships in Osaka, Japan. Unfortunately, few Canadians noticed, because there was little or no television coverage of the event here in Canada. Four years earlier, the championships were broadcast in prime time for seven straight days.

At the 2008 World Figure Skating Championships in Sweden, Jeffrey Buttle became the first Canadian skater to win gold since Elvis Stojko in 1997. But the only Western Canadians who noticed were the insomniacs who may have come across a two-hour telecast at midnight local time.

And to think that in the mid-1990s, an era with only one all-sports channel, the national championships for sports like rowing, track and field, figure skating, and swimming often attracted national attention.

With the OTP and RTE programs now the driving force in Canada, the Olympics are the new mantra in sport — everything else is secondary. Events like the Commonwealth Games, the third-largest international sporting event in the world; the World Cup of Soccer, the second-largest international sporting event in the world; and the World Baseball Classic have meekly given way to the Olympics.

The net result is a sport system driven by an organization interested in Olympic sport not amateur sport.

Consider the sport of baseball, an Olympic sport at the 2008 Games and one, according to Sport Canada, with more than a million registered participants across the country. Because baseball was part of the Olympic movement in 2008, the sport received nearly $1,000,000 in government funding in 2007-2008. Unfortunately, baseball will be removed from the Olympic roster in

2012. Yet the game, in the years to come, will continue to be an integral component of amateur sport in Canada. In fact, Canadians competed for a medal at the 2009 World Baseball Classic. However, the RTE and the COC fail to see the importance of a non-Olympic event. As a result, it is widely known that in the quadrennial to come, baseball will see its funding slashed.

Baseball isn't alone. For example, football, squash, and water skiing — sports that are extremely popular in Canada, according to a Sport Canada report — are all expected to see substantial cuts in funding in the years to come. Why? Because they aren't contested at the Olympics.

"We've been seeing non-Olympic sports become increasingly marginalized in the Canadian sport system and the gap is absolutely widening," says Water Ski and Wakeboard Canada executive director Dan Wolfenden.

Meanwhile, rowing, a sport with slightly less than sixteen thousand registered participants in Canada, but part of the Olympic movement, is expected to benefit enormously, to the tune of $3.2 million per annum in government funding between 2009 and 2012.

Who is overseeing sport?

In 2001, Alex Baumann, then a high-ranking official in Australia's sport program, wrote a scathing letter to Canada's sport administrators. In it he detailed the problems facing our sport program. "Lack of vision among administrators and decision-makers has, for too long, produced mediocrity. Canada needs to critically analyse performances at all levels and have the will to fix the system, something that has eluded it so far." Some seven years later, with Baumann now overseeing sport in Canada as opposed to criticizing it, the challenges he faces to resurrect a sport system are perhaps even more daunting.

He enters into a sporting system now headed by Gary Lunn, the disgraced minister for natural resources, whose handling of the Chalk River nuclear reactor led to calls from Opposition MPs for his immediate resignation. Given the succession of ministers with no proven experience in sport, Baumann asks, "Who's driving the bus in Canada?" Trevino Betty, a director with the Commonwealth Games Federation of Canada, goes a step further when he says that the government's present involvement within sport is a waste of time.

The OTP and RTE programs were created by the COC with the sole purpose of getting Canadians on the podium at the Olympic Games, and thereby burnishing the Olympic image in Canada. But as Pat Fiacco, mayor of the city of Regina, points out, "We can Own the Podium today, but who is going to Own the Podium in 2016?" Fortunately for Canada's winter athletes, WinSport, with assistance from the Olympic Oval in Calgary, acknowledges the seriousness of that question and is trying to develop novice, amateur, and professional athletes alike. In contrast, if you're not an elite athlete in one of the sports contested at the Olympics — that is if you're one of the millions of Canadians involved in a panoply of summer sports — you're left out in the cold. Who *is* driving the bus?

Mark Lowry, an executive director with the Canadian Olympics Committee, notes that, with the implementation of the Road to Excellence/Own the Podium programs, a council of sport experts had been formed so the people who do sports can tell the bureaucrats who oversee the organizations which policies work and which need to be scrapped.

But under the present system, no one is overseeing amateur sport. Canada's sport system is focused on the Olympic Games and Olympic success. Even the COC itself acknowledges this state of affairs. "The government can have their focus on health care and general well-being, but the COC message remains intact," says COC communications manager Stacie Smith. "We're trying to get funding to create a better sports system ... for podium finishes."

Interestingly, however, when it comes to funding, the COC is quick to advocate the general well-being of sport. In a submission to the House of Commons in search of enhanced funding, the head of the RTE plan argued that an investment in sport promoted the benefits of a healthy society in reducing health-care costs. "I think they understand what we're saying," notes Alex Baumann. "The critical point is to (align) the health of Canadians with active lifestyles — it would take a burden off the health budget if more Canadians were involved in sport."

Earlier, upon his return from Australia to lead the RTE Olympic program, Baumann said, "For a long time post 1988, particularly in the sports system, we didn't really focus on excellence; we were more interested in just partici-pation. I believe very strongly we should strive to be the best that we can in the world."

Canadians agree, but wonder if their country couldn't strike a better balance between sport and Olympic glory.

Ken Read, CEO of Alpine Canada, thinks so, saying that "the Canadian Olympic Committee is focused on excellence, not on ... problems with the sport system that produces candidates for excellence." He adds that athletes at the grass-roots level go without proper coaching, sport science support, travel assistance, and other elements linked to performance because of the COC's unending commitment to high-performance sport.

Mark Greenwald, a former U.S. Olympic speed skater, thinks Canada would benefit from employing a U.S. model by which "America doesn't send athletes to the Olympic Games, Americans do." One hundred percent of all funding for high-performance amateur sport in the U.S. is financed through the country's Olympic Committee (USOC), he says, which raises funds through corporate sponsorship. Meanwhile, government agencies are focused on placing resources on developing sport at the grass-roots level.

Comparing Canadian and American sport systems is difficult, given the disparity in population between the two countries. Not so when it comes to comparing the Canadian and Australian systems.

PART THREE

Pointing the Way
to Summer Success

9

The Aussie Touch: A Case Study

Despite the new quad's limited practice as a crew, their odds of success were good. There were only seven boats, three of which would win a medal. Tracy's boat was one of four that had a legitimate chance of winning gold.

With Tracy's fiancé Mark Duk in attendance, Canada's lightweight women's quad won world championship gold in Japan, breaking the world record in the process. Tracy was now a world champion, sparking the beginning of an incredible year-long run.

Money was no longer an issue. Not only was Tracy about to be carded — which would lead to a $1,500-per-month tax-free salary — she also was about to secure sponsorship agreements with oil and gas giants Midnight Oil and Daylight Energy Resource Trust.

With love and money in place, marriage was soon to follow. In January 2006, in Banff, Alberta, in front of a who's who of the rowing world, Tracy and Mark made a lifelong commitment to each other. However, with Mark's job in Calgary, and the national rowing centre located in Victoria, the two agreed to live in separate cities — for the time being. Mark was hoping to take a one-year sabbatical from his job in 2007 to be closer to his wife, and take his master's degree at the University of Victoria. Until then, weekend visits would be the norm.

The only thing missing in Tracy's life at the time was stability, and that, too, was forthcoming. Al Morrow, the head coach of the women's national rowing team, was stepping down from his duties to assume a development role in the organization. Laryssa Biesenthal, a two-time Olympic medallist, was assuming the coaching duties of the lightweight women's team. With the coaching change, it was agreed that Victoria was to become the full-time home of Canada's lightweight women's rowing program, ending the cross-country moves to London. Like most everyday Canadians, Tracy was employed in one location.

Interesting things happen when personal matters are taken care of. With money, stability, and love come happiness, and happiness often translates into success. By May 2006, Tracy's life was living proof of this phenomenon. She was happier than she had ever been and more success-ful than ever before on the rowing circuit. At a world cup that May, she won gold in the lightweight women's single. The single was a non-Olympic event, but her result served notice that she was ready to take on all comers in the most prestigious of lightweight events, the women's double.

By June, Tracy was back rowing the double with Mara. With time to finally practise together, things started clicking. By July, the two were rowing in perfect unison — from a distance they looked as one. Their results spoke for themselves.

Returning to Lucerne in 2006 — now with a new partner in Mara and accustomed to the distractions of international rowing — Tracy and her partner shocked the world. They won the lightweight women's double in their first-ever international race together. In one seven-minute race, international lightweight women's rowing had been turned upside down. For the first time in over ten years, a Canadian crew was heading into the world championships favoured to win gold. And with those championships still nearly two months away, the pair was more confident than ever. They could only get faster.

~

And the gold goes to ... the Australian program! They win in the pool, on the track, and in the gym. And after each successive victory their followers chant, in unison, Aussie, Aussie, Aussie, Oi, Oi, Oi! Everywhere people turned at the 2000 Olympic Games, people were raising the chant again and again, each time more enthusiastically than the last. It went on for two weeks straight as Australian after Australian reached Olympic success.

Four years later in Athens, after the world had finally forgotten the rather simple rhythm, the Australians started it up again. At diving and swimming, at running and jumping, at gymnastics, badminton, and even synchronized swimming, Australians were again rejoicing in their country's athletic prowess.

Today, the chant is almost impossible to escape as the country's athletes flex their summer supremacy all over the world. From the Olympic Games to rugby and now even soccer, where the country shocked the world by finishing in the top sixteen at the 2006 world cup before losing to eventual champion Italy, Australia is a summer sporting power that is feared the world over.

At the 2000 Olympics, the country, with a population of 20 million, came fourth in the overall medals race after the United States, Russia, and China with populations of 300 million, 142 million, and 1.3 billion respectively. Australia became the first country to maintain the same high ranking after playing host, retaining fourth place overall to those same three countries at the Athens Games in 2004. In Beijing, they nearly did it again, coming fifth in the overall medal count, losing out to those same three countries and finishing one medal behind Great Britain. Not bad for a country that ranks fifty-fourth in the world in population.

Remove those amateur sport superpowers of China, Russia, and the United States from the equation (as is the case at the Commonwealth Games, a competition confined to British Commonwealth nations) and Australia's sporting domination becomes all the more impressive. Not only has Australia topped the medal standings at the last five Commonwealth Games, it has also increased its medal haul over the last twenty years. After finishing third to Canada and England at the 1978 Games, Australia won more medals than England and Canada combined in 2006, proving just how dominant the country has become. In 2006, Australia, with only 1.6 percent of the Commonwealth's total population, won over 30 percent of the medals awarded.

A fall from grace

"Our Olympic Flop Will Continue Unless ... ," "Canadians Turn Tables on Us," "Australia's Golden Days Have Gone."

These were some of the headlines in Australia following the country's flop at the 1976 Olympics. With a meagre five medals and not one of them gold in the country's worst Olympic performance in over forty years, Australia felt its national pride had been insulted. A country that had been accustomed to success at past Summer Olympic Games was now faltering. Enraged citizens demanded answers. Australian athletes and coaches wanted action. Sport officials demanded money, while the federal government reminded citizens that the Olympics were about more than medals.

Australia's failure shouldn't have surprised anyone. The Olympic Games were becoming serious business for countries around the world, which were devoting substantial resources toward the development of athletes. Meanwhile, the lack of an obvious portfolio related to sport within the federal government and a turnstile of ministers managing numerous duties to which athletics had been included only reinforced the sorry state of affairs.

Two years later, at the 1978 Commonwealth Games in Edmonton, Alberta, Australia's sporting problems resurfaced once again when the country's athletes finished far behind Canada in the medal tally. It would be the last such time that Canada would beat Australia in the overall medal tally at either a Commonwealth Games or a non-boycotted Summer Olympic Games.

Full-court press

Following Australia's debacle in Montreal, a series of new initiatives would soon bring major improvements: financial support and governance for athletes, construction of public and high-performance facilities, and access to better coaching and technology. One of the first of these undertakings was the development of sporting facilities across the country. Recognizing that the country's athletic facilities were old and outdated, the government introduced a matching grants program with state and municipal governments. With funding from all three levels of government, recreation centres began to spring up throughout the country. As John Bloomfield reports, "Once the centres were constructed, the management of them was assumed by local governments, enabling local areas to establish more varied sport and recreation programs as well as use of the facilities for physical fitness activities."

Australian sport authorities then turned their attention to developing high-performance sporting facilities for the 1982 Commonwealth Games in Brisbane, Australia. The Games were an international success and left the country with a legacy of competition. And they helped kick-start the development of high-performance athletic venues across the country, a trend that continued until the start of the Sydney Games in 2000. These venues are used by high-performing athletes to this day.

But Australians weren't satisfied with the proliferation of high-performance and recreation facilities across the country. They demanded that a modern system be developed from top to bottom. After years of frustration in seeing sport relegated to second-tier status, lobby groups intensified their demands. In 1978, hearing the calls for a sporting resurgence, the government finally recognized that a high-ranking politician with a love for sport was required to assume the sport portfolio. The incumbent was former attorney general Bob Ellicott, who realized the importance of sport in the lives of Australians and helped foster its development. An able politician with the ability to foster change, Ellicott transformed Australian sport, through the introduction of the Australian Institute for Sport (AIS).

Ellicott had long argued that a sport institute would produce sporting stars who would do Australia proud internationally. Sceptics argued otherwise, but with his enthusiasm for the project and previous record within the government, Ellicott won over the prime minister. On Australia Day, January 26, 1981, the PM officially opened the doors to the Australia Institute of Sport in Canberra, Australia, proclaiming, "Australia is no longer going to let the rest of the world pass us by."

The newly established institute opened with the intention that Australia's best male and female athletes could be trained to reach their full potential. Some 153 of Australia's best athletes across eight different sports were invited to Canberra in that inaugural year with that very idea in mind. With athletes from the sports of basketball, gymnastics, netball, soccer, swimming, tennis, and track and field, the AIS incorporated a full range of sporting activities that Australians considered important. The sports (according to figures released by the Australian government) all had high rates of participation among Australian citizens. However, the eight sports selected weren't necessarily the country's most prolific. For example, netball has never been contested at an Olympic Games. Australia has never won an Olympic medal in soccer and didn't win its first medal in basketball until 1996. Australia has since won four medals in the latter sport — all of them by their women.

Using the eight foundation sports as their base and with a focus on long-term athlete development within these sports, Australia's success began to spill over into other disciplines. Over time, AIS gradually expanded its program base to reflect its success across a broad spectrum of activities. It now offers scholarships to seven hundred athletes in twenty-six different sports.

From those early days, when Australia's best athletes were invited to eat, sleep, and train at some of the country's best athletic facilities, the AIS transformed itself into a breeding ground for Olympic champions, becoming arguably the greatest sporting institution of its kind. Pierre Lafontaine, former AIS swim coach and now CEO of Swimming Canada, says that AIS created an "expectation of performance."

Applying the best technology the world has to offer and using a team of experts in medicine, biomechanics, and other applied sciences, all working together for the betterment of sport, AIS provided athletes with a more informed body of knowledge. Encouraging international athletes to train within the confines of AIS helped Australian athletes see that they could compete with the world's best.

The AIS also stressed the importance of high coach-to-athlete ratios, giving athletes the resources they needed, and thus contributing to the improvement of sport performance throughout the country. Not surprisingly, eleven years after AIS first opened its doors, Australian athletes won nearly 500 percent more medals at the 1992 Olympic Games than in 1976.

But the idea behind AIS was not just to develop athletes; it was also to develop coaches. Hiring the best coaches from around the world and putting them all in one location allowed them to share best practices. According to Lafontaine, the high quality of coaching in Australia is what sets its program apart from others around the world. "There are a huge number of foreign coaches at AIS who bring practices and processes from around the globe into the Australian system," he says. "The volleyball team is coached by an Argentinian, the swim team by Aussies and Canadians, the cycling team by a Brit, all of whom bring expertise into the system."

Information gradually passed on from the coaches at the AIS to the sport associations themselves, thereby enhancing the level of coaching throughout the country. With the improvement of the athletes and the input of the AIS coaches, national sport organizations began hiring national directors of coaching for the task of coaching the coaches. The result was a highly professional coaching fraternity from the national sport associations down to the states themselves.

Those insatiable Aussies! Despite the effect AIS was having on its coaches and athletes alike, they continued to demand more from their sport system. They were demanding a professionalized sport system not just at the national level but also at the local level.

As the size and scope of AIS gradually increased and Australian high-performance sport became more and more centralized, state governments began calling for a decentralization of AIS into the states. It had become obvious to the states farthest away from Canberra that young elite athletes were not able or did not want to leave their homes and relocate to AIS. These states started developing their own institutes. Operating in isolation, these institutes began to compete with AIS in attracting high-calibre athletes. With four state or territory institutes in operation by the mid 1980s, it was clear that more coordination was needed between AIS and the state institutes if the Australian sport system was to reach its full potential on into the twenty-first century.

An enlightened move

The importance of a coordinated sport program with strong central leadership was becoming more and more evident. Sport experts argued that what sport needed now was its own voice with its own controlling body, decreasing political interference as much as possible. Manned by high-ranking individuals with proven sport backgrounds, a new statutory authority known as the Australian Sports Commission (ASC) was created in 1984. Independent of government, the ASC had the ear of the minister of sport and the prime minister. This was an enlightened move, demonstrating that the government didn't want to control sport's highest executive body and would accept that body's informed decisions.

One of the ASC's first initiatives was to increase sport participation among school-aged children. Educators and coaches had long argued that many Australian sports were too complicated, the fields and courts too large, and the equipment too heavy for young children. Concerned with low participation in sport and high obesity rates among primary school kids, the Aussie Sport Organization was formed in 1986. Its mandate was to develop modified rules for children across the country in more than thirty sports. In addition, it established coaching and awards programs for various sports and appointed coordinators for the various states. Since those early days, Aussie Sport has grown to the point where it is now incorporated into all of the primary schools across Australia, with 2.5 million children competing in modified sport activities each year.

The ASC was equally concerned with elite athletes, making it known that one of its basic objectives was to improve Australia's performance in international sport. To achieve its targets, the ASC sought to create more links with AIS and the state institutes, recognizing that a high level of cooperation was required if Australia was to reach its full potential as a sporting nation. In 1993, after Sydney secured the bid to host the 2000 Olympics, the emphasis on federal-state cooperation kicked into high gear with the creation of the National Elite Sports Council (NESC). Consisting of directors from AIS, ASC, and the seven state institutes, this council brought all of Australia's stakeholders together with the purpose of creating a coordinated sporting system while delivering quality sport programs. Through the establishment of the NESC in 1994, the Australian sport model changed from competition to cooperation between AIS and the state institutes.

The result was a national network of sophisticated training institutes accountable to the ASC, notes Alex Baumann. Baumann says that as the executive director of the Queensland Academy of Sport, he met with the heads of AIS, ASC, and the state institutes semi-annually to go over, among other things, key performance indicators from the athletes right through to the coaches. The establishment of objectives in turn created what Baumann calls "a lot of accountability."

"I had twenty-six coaches across twenty-one sports under contract with me, all of whom were on two- to four-year contracts," Baumann says. "If they didn't perform, they were let go." But accountability didn't end with the coaches. Baumann adds that he was accountable to the ASC, which made it known to him that his objectives were to have Queensland athletes make up 20 to 25 percent of the national team, and 20 to 25 percent of Olympic medallists from the country. With responsibility placed squarely on his shoulders, he had the authority to intervene in a sports program if things weren't running properly and dictate how it should operate.

In this system, each of the respective institutes, under incredible pressure to perform, chooses, through the recommendations of the coaches who serve them, the services it wishes to provide its athletes. And with a number of development pathways available, each offering an array of services, it is Australia's athlete who benefits.

Kurtis MacGillivary, a Canadian swimmer on scholarship at the Queensland Academy of Sport, acknowledges the success of the Aussie system. "They do everything for you here. Swim trips are paid for ... I have access to physio, massage, and nutritionists. Everything is covered." The result, he says, is that "you get better here." The results speak for themselves. MacGillivary points out that during his three years in Australia prior to the 2004 Games, he took a minute off his time in the 1500m freestyle.

By the time the 2000 Sydney Olympics had started, everything was in place for a historic performance. But unforeseen by most was just how well they would do: medals in twenty sports, and 128 top-eight performances. Australia was finally given its due. After a twenty-four-year resurgence following that low point in Montreal, Australia was recognized as a major sporting power.

The lessons for Canada

It is a sporting triumph that the nations of the world want to copy, Canada included. By throwing bucket-loads of money at Australia's sporting hierarchy, luring Alex Baumann to oversee Canada's Road to Excellence program, and appointing Pierre Lafontaine as CEO of Swimming Canada, Canada hopes to replicate Australia's sporting success. There's no reason why it can't. The two countries have similar governments, similar people, and closely linked economies.

However, the results of the 2008 Olympic Games show just how far Canada has to go to compete with Australia. At the 2008 Olympic Games, Australia won forty-six medals and came home questioning why it didn't win more. Canada's medal haul in Beijing, meanwhile, was just over one-third of that. Disappointing when you consider that Canada's GDP ($1.178 trillion) is nearly twice that of its Commonwealth neighbour ($674 billion). Disappointing, but not unexpected.

Canada should have learned from the past that simply luring Australia's athletic brain trust to come north doesn't automatically mean global athletic glory. After the 2000 Olympics, famed Australian rowing coach Brian Richardson was hired to oversee Canada's rowing team. The purpose of his return was to bring new direction to a rowing program that won only one medal at the 2000 Summer Games. Richardson was also asked to help oversee the COC's then $8.7-million Excellence Fund, a fund, according to the COC, that was to "enable our Olympic athletes to perform successfully and consistently on the world stage." Unfortunately for Canadians, both Canada's rowing program and its Summer Olympic program failed to meet expectations in Athens.

If we funded our athletes the way Australia does, we'd be winning medals, too, Canadian sport officials say in defending their performance at the Summer Games. However, the amounts the countries give are roughly equal. In 2003, the government of Australia contributed $134 million to the departmental agency responsible for amateur sport funding in Australia; in 2006, the Canadian government contributed over $155 million toward amateur sport.

Another argument trotted out is that Australia focuses solely on the sports that they are good at while Canada tries to be everything to everyone. But Australia has long recognized the cross-training aspects of sport, which is why it provides nearly $400,000 in direct funding to organizations like Surf Lifesaving Australia. With over 100,000 members in 275 clubs across Australia, surf lifesaving has produced some of Australia's most prominent Olympians in swimming, triathlon, and kayaking. Furthermore, it is Australia's new approach, through exchange programs with Asian sport teams in badminton, table tennis, judo, baseball, softball, and taekwondo, to go after medals in all disciplines. Canada's new approach, meanwhile, is to specialize in a limited number of activities by pouring money into those sports with proven success.

Canada focuses exclusively on hockey and American professional leagues, we tell ourselves. However, Australia has even more problems in this regard. The national game is cricket. The next three most popular sports are rugby union, rugby league, and don't forget Aussie Rules. Soccer and basketball are more popular in Australia than they are in Canada, while surfing is a cultural phenomenon.

After all the issues are analysed, the cold hard facts remain. As Ken MacQueen noted in a *Maclean's* article, following the 1976 Olympics in Montreal, both Canada and Australia returned home with disappointing finishes. Australia committed resources and political will to rebuild a sporting power. Canada has bumbled along with bandages and bureaucratic studies.

Says Baumann, who helped oversee Australia's sport system from 1991 to 2006, Australia today "has a coordinated and integrated approach ... where all the stakeholders ... are on the same page, dedicated to the same goal." The result is a system that maximizes efficiency in the delivery of services to the athletes and ensures accountability for every dollar spent.

Baumann returned home from Australia as Canada's white knight in 2006, becoming the executive director of the Road to Excellence program. In an interview with *Northern Life*, Baumann noted that an Australian type of system exists only for Canada's winter athletes. "On the winter side ... there's incredible movement. The results from Torino 2006 were a confidence booster for our athletes. Summer side, it isn't there. At this point and time there's no coordinated or integrated system for summer sports ... We have to maximize efficiency with our resources. We're not there yet, but we will be."

Canada has a good reason to believe him. Baumann is serious about implementing change within the Canadian summer sport system. However, to create the change that both Baumann and Canadians expect, a number of things have to happen that will take time and energy. After all, it took Australia more than fifteen years before results were seen.

Fortunately, Canada can benefit from studying the Australian system. It can reduce the lag time before seeing results. However, as Marvin Washington notes, Canada cannot simply copy the Australian system because 80 percent of the Canadian sport system is directly influenced by the sporting juggernaut south of the country's border. Australian athletes, thousands of kilometres from the U.S., aren't as influenced as Canadian athletes by an American sports media to compete in the high-glamour, high-stress world of U.S. collegiate athletics.

The importance of leadership

While Canada has to develop a made-in-Canada approach to amateur sport, one thing we can take from the Australian system is the importance of effective leadership, which is lacking here.

The current individual in charge of sport within the federal government doesn't have the authority to get things approved. The coc doesn't have the ability to fund sport. And the Road to Excellence, while classified as independent, is a branch of the coc and isn't concerned with anything but Canada's performance at the Olympics.

"What we need is an independent group of sports experts with no financial interest, and no vested interest to manage sport ... who can persuade the government," says Bob Storey, president of the International Bobsleigh and Skeleton Federation.

"We need a sport minister who can get things approved," says Jim Christie of the *Globe and Mail*.

Right now neither situation exists, something even the COC acknowledges when its CEO says, "We need leadership from the top."

To get the sort of leadership that the COC and Canada's sport experts seemingly beg for, Canada will have to separate sport from government. "There is no reason to have Sport Canada ... (It) is a bureaucracy that presents another set of hurdles that one has to navigate," says Storey. IOC member Paul Henderson agrees, saying that Canada's sport system needs to get rid of the bureaucrats.

A sport system void of government interference exists within the Australian Sports Commission. Canada should follow the lead of its commonwealth neighbour and implement a similar organization with equally broad powers. The body should consist of high-ranking sport officials, be void of political and outside interference, and have the ear of a sports minister with the ability to accept and act on their decisions.

This would be an enlightened move. It would eliminate much of the bureaucracy that plagues Canada's sporting system and make everyone accountable for their actions. Such a system would benefit both Canada's Summer and Winter Olympic athletes and be a valuable first step in creating a powerful amateur sports program.

10

Melting the Ice: Creating a Culture of Sport

*When the work of rowing was done for the day, dinner, a coffee, a movie,
and sometimes even a beer were on the agenda, giving Tracy and her
fellow rowers time to analyse the day's activities.*

*Relationships that amateur athletes form with one another are special
ones that few can comprehend. Athletes don't work in the hierarchical
structure that most Canadians experience in their jobs. Everyone is on
equal footing, the pay is virtually the same, and everyone is striving for
the same goal: to become an Olympic champion.*

*Because of their similarities, male and female athletes alike under-
stand one another. They understand the strain that athletics can cause,
the pressures of competitive life, the financial struggles, and the constant
criticism from coaches. As a result, conversations are easy, and time together
(virtually every waking moment) is enjoyable.*

*Meanwhile, back home in Calgary, many of Tracy's friends thought
she was hiding from the real world: that it was time for her to move on
with her life and get a "real job." Time to find a career and have kids.
Her teammates, on the other hand, understood that rowing was her job*

and that it was, in many ways, more important than any other profession in the country. She was working to represent all Canadians at the Olympic Games and in the process to defend the pride of her country.

Over time, her reliance on friends back home began to fade while her relationships with fellow athletes continued to build. And this was beginning to have an effect on her marriage.

Mark's life in the oil patch was progressing nicely, while Tracy's life in the rowing world was falling apart. Tracy and Mara finished out of the medals at the 2006 world championships, coming in fourth. Shortly thereafter, Mara had informed Rowing Canada that she was quitting rowing to go to medical school. Tracy would have to start over and find a new rowing partner in 2007.

By December 2006, Mark and Tracy were growing apart. The two had worked hard to keep their relationship strong, but Tracy lived in Victoria, Mark was still in Calgary, and their lives were on completely different paths. They decided to call it quits.

~

Canada's winter athletes have long been celebrated the world over for their athletic accomplishments. In hockey, Howe, Orr, Lafleur, Gretzky, Lemieux, and now Crosby are names that are synonymous with the game around the world, while a Canadian named Wickenheiser became the first woman in the world to play hockey in a men's professional league.

In figure skating, Canada's successes are equally well known. Jeffrey Buttle retired in 2008 at the very top of his game. Kurt Browning not only is a four-time world champion in the sport, he is also the first in the world to have landed a quadruple jump in competition. Brian Orser, a two-time Olympic medallist, was the first to land a triple axel at the Olympic Games. Elvis Stojko, a world champion and also two-time Olympic silver-medallist, was the first to land a quad-double and quad-triple combination in competition.

In skiing, Canada's Crazy Canucks of the 1970s and 1980s earned a world-wide reputation for a fast, almost reckless approach to their sport, while the name Nancy Greene is securely linked to the sport. Think cross-country skiing and Olympic gold medallist Beckie Scott quickly comes to mind. Scott now sits on the IOC athletes' council and is an international advocate for drug-free sport. In speed skating and curling, Canada is a world superpower where podium finishes are expected.

Dale Henwood, president of the Canadian Sport Centre in Calgary, says that this phenomenon exists because Canada is a "winter nation."

Olympic gold medallist Daniel Igali agrees, saying that there is a "winter culture here in Canada."

Winter mythology

Marvin Washington, a professor at the University of Alberta, disagrees. "It is a myth that Canada is a winter sport nation," he says. "But if something is portrayed as true, it is believed by others to be true."

This myth is perpetuated by the fact that indoor and outdoor skating arenas litter the sports landscape in Canada, while summer sports facilities are scarce and in a state of disrepair. The myth is fuelled by a hockey-crazed society where hockey dominates the sports headlines and parents put kids in year-round high-performance programs, hoping to raise the next Jarome Iginla, Dany Heatley, or Steve Yzerman. Meanwhile, sports like baseball, basketball, football, and soccer are seen to hold little opportunity for Canadians because they are dominated by Americans. As a result, these sports are seen as a haven for parents who consider hockey too competitive, too rough, and too intense for their children.

Yet, aside from the Olympics, Canadians aren't interested in bobsleigh, luge, skeleton, long track speed skating, ski jumping, or even freestyle skiing. Nor do we have the infrastructure in Canada to support these events from coast to coast. To suggest otherwise, try thinking of ten Canadians outside the sports of hockey, figure skating, and curling who competed at the 2006 Olympics. Try thinking of a location outside Alberta — and now Vancouver/ Whistler, too — where it's possible to take part in any of these activities.

What we have is a hockey culture, where hockey dominates Canadian sports from October through April. In the winter months, seemingly every Canadian kid across the country goes to the local rink and laces up a pair of skates, dreaming of emulating the local hero who plays professional hockey. These kids are in turn assisted by a sports system that has the infrastructure to support their development. This gives young athletes the confidence that if they want to realize their dream, they can do it in their own country. And while not every one of these kids will go on to play in the NHL or the WWHL (Western Women's Hockey League), many will develop the cross-training benefits for other Winter Olympic sports. Washington points out that this is why Canada succeeds on the Winter Olympic scene.

Consider the case of Jamie Gregg. Following in the footsteps of his father, Randy, an ex-NHLer, Jamie played junior B hockey before he was identified through the Own the Podium recruitment program in 2004. Understanding the cross-training benefits of hockey, the OTP recruitment program identified him as a potential medallist at the 2010 Games in the sport of long track speed skating. After only a few short years in the sport, Jamie is the (2008) men's national champion in the 500m and is representing Canada on the world cup circuit in 2009.

Alex Gardiner, the then senior director Olympic programming with the COC, certainly agrees that hockey raises the bar in other winter sports. "A higher tide floats all boats," he says.

Perhaps this explains why Canada's Summer Olympians are struggling. There is no sport on the summer side of the equation that raises the bar for the other sports. Nor is there a development process for summer sports.

It becomes harder to establish a development base with the Road to Excellence program continuing to funnel money to the less visible but successful summer activities like rowing and trampoline for the sole purpose of Olympic glory. Not a lot of kids in Canada are going to row, regardless of whether Canada is successful in that sport at the Olympic Games. The sport simply isn't visible to the Canadian public.

Meanwhile, the visible sports of basketball, soccer, boxing, and volleyball are slipping into oblivion. "Kids in Canada are exposed to ten to twelve different sports before they are twelve years old," notes Washington. "In the United States they are teaching track and field, basketball, soccer, and football ... cheap and easy sports that are popular with kids because the U.S wins in these disciplines."

High school basketball and football are so popular in the U.S., says Washington, that the captain of the football or basketball team is often named the high school homecoming king.

There is some evidence to suggest that this phenomenon exists in Canada, most notably in Quebec, where kids want to play Canadian football and college games are now attracting larger crowds than did the now defunct Expos baseball team. Football teams in la belle province are thriving as a result. University teams from Quebec have won four of the last five Vanier Cups, the Canadian university/college football championship. For the most part, however, football and basketball are relatively unknown across the country. Those talented enough often move to the U.S., leaving Canadians to wonder why they should follow these sports in Canada when the best Canadian kids are south of the border.

"If we want to truly encourage the development of Canada's Summer Olympic system, Canada has to find a way to make the sports of soccer, football, and basketball popular with the Canadian public," says Washington. That means improving the development opportunities in these sports. We have to get Canadian kids to aspire to play in the CFL or (w)NBA or the w-league in women's soccer. Over time, improvement within these sports will translate to increased opportunities in other athletic disciplines, which is where programs like RTE should focus their efforts.

A cash cow

The Road to Excellence program is due to receive $72 million in federal monies from 2009 to 2012. This is over and above the $55 million the government has given to the OTP program, the $140 million it gives annually to Sport Canada (the governmental agency overseeing amateur sport in Canada), and the over $600 million needed to finance the cost of staging the 2010 Olympics.

"But what if the government provided no money?" asks Washington. "Some sports will fail, others will thrive." All of which, he notes, would create a sport system that had its own targeted funding structure like that of the RTE and OTP programs but without any government intervention.

Bob Barney, the founding director of the International Centre for Olympic

Studies, doesn't disagree, noting that athletic improvement programs should be financed privately.

On the Canadian sport landscape today, high-performance sports that connect with the Canadian public (like alpine skiing, ice hockey, basketball, and soccer) derive a significant portion of their revenues from corporate sponsors and registered participants, whereas an organization like Rowing Canada relies on government for over 85 percent of its annual revenues. All of this creates inefficiencies in the system. Canadians who enjoy activities like hockey and soccer are being asked to reallocate their tax dollars — at the expense of well-known high-performing athletes within their sport of choice — to fund an unknown few in sports like rowing.

But while Washington suggests that the government should remove itself from the financing of high-performance sport, he recognizes that it has to support some sports at the development level. "We lived in Chicago, and throughout the region, government supports some but not all sports," he says. He explains how all three levels of government (municipal, state, and federal) have helped fund a program known as Midnight Basketball not only to help channel inner city youths' energy but also to develop an upcoming generation of high-performing athletes.

Midnight Basketball, originally designed to get inner city youth off America's streets with basketball games between 10 p.m. and 2 a.m., has become a nation-wide phenomenon. Watched by over two hundred thousand Americans a night, ten thousand kids between the ages of fifteen and twenty-five now play organized basketball three to four times per week across fifty U.S cities. Those talented enough are later offered scholarships by top colleges. The best players then go on to play professional basketball in the NBA or in overseas leagues.

But while some U.S. basketball players will take their skills to professional leagues, others will apply them to other sports. Athletes like Roy Jones Jr., for example. He played semi-pro basketball but is more famously known for having won Olympic silver in the sport of boxing at the 1992 Olympics prior to becoming the world's best pound-for-pound fighter. Or like Dan Beery. Beery played two years of college basketball for Bryan College prior to winning an Olympic gold medal in the sport of rowing in 2004. Or like four-time Olympic medallist Lenny Krayzelburg, who played high school hoops prior to garnering Olympic glory in the pool. Pole-vaulter Jenn Stuczynski won a silver medal at the Beijing Games a little over four years removed from a promising career as a collegiate basketball player. The list goes on and therein lies the problem with Canadian summer sport, says Washington. "There isn't a developmental sport within Canada to produce high-calibre summer athletes."

And as he points out, before we can have high-performing athletes in these sports, we need to develop facilities to encourage development in these sports. Dr. Bruce Kidd, dean of the faculty of physical education and health at the University of Toronto, agrees. "The need for a dedicated federal-provincial/territorial sport, physical activity, and recreation infrastructure program is an essential component of our capacity to realize the goals of Canadian sport policy, both for high-performance sport and broadly based opportunities."

Building from the ground up

"Opportunities for high-performing athletes come from the building up of the community," says Ian Bird, senior leader with the Sport Matters Group. This is a reality that many acknowledge but few outside of WinSport Canada are prepared to tackle.

Mark Keast of the *Globe and Mail* reports that "it is widely acknowledged that Canadians are increasingly struggling with obesity and other health complications associated with inactivity, in the process seriously taxing our national health-care system. The Conference Board of Canada states that health-care spending caused by physical inactivity ranges from $2.1 billion to $5.3 billion annually."

Silken Laumann, athlete, author, and now advocate for active families, notes that children, for healthy growth and development, need to be moderately or vigorously active for at least ninety minutes a day. According to Statistics Canada, only 43 percent of children meet that minimum standard, while 26 percent are either overweight or obese.

In the face of such discouraging figures, the federal government's response is the return of Participaction, a federally funded program to promote physical fitness. And this despite concerns inside Health Canada that it could mean millions of misspent dollars.

Liberal MP Denis Coderre, who regretted the loss of the program in 2001 when he was minister of amateur sport, says, "At the end, the way it was working, it was not working at all. But you need a Participaction."

Do we? In a submission to the Commons committee, Laumann noted that politicians need to create a coast-to-coast "backyard Olympics," one where "what matters is not how fast you run or how strong you are, but how many minutes you spend skipping or playing kick-the-can."

She says this can be achieved by finding a way to propagate successful programs that already exist in a number of communities across the country. This in turn is done by hiring coordinators in various regions who provide basic information and backing this effort with a marketing campaign pegged to the 2010 Olympics.

A model similar to the one employed by WinSport.

Filling the gap

WinSport's impact is felt not only by Canada's high-performing athletes but also by all sport enthusiasts. WinSport, unlike any other organization in the world, not only manages and maintains the facilities from the 1988 Games, it also allows the facilities to function as a multi-purpose competition, training, and recreation area designed for year-round use by both athletes and the public.

In the winter months, Canada Olympic Park (cop) is home to nearly 300,000 ski and snowboard visits each year, making it the second largest snow academy in Canada. cop offers lessons for people of all ages and abilities in all of its sports. cop also offers introductory programs for the public to experience the exciting sports of bobsleigh, skeleton, and luge. John Mills, a former president of WinSport, notes that giving the public access to the facilities creates a made-in-Canada solution to sport, since it is the public that is helping to fund high-performance sport. Furthermore, Mills adds, allowing the public to use the facilities doesn't take away from the training needs of Canada's high-performing athletes, since they typically train during non-peak hours. It is this type of cost-sharing arrangement that has allowed WinSport to manage the day-to-day operations of the facility for the past twenty years without taking a dime of Canadian taxpayers' money.

Thanks to a landmark agreement in 2006 with the Calgary Board of Education, WinSport will continue to promote sport to the public in the years ahead. This unique and innovative relationship is designed to promote active living through physical education programs at WinSport's Canada Olympic Park and at the Canmore Nordic Centre. In 2006 alone, WinSport introduced nearly 100,000 students representing 215 schools to winter sport activities in Calgary. Today, students in the Calgary area can participate in a wide array of recreational winter and summer activities at COP, including alpine and nordic skiing, snowboarding, snowshoeing, mountain biking, hiking, and orienteering.

"Increased sport participation will significantly reduce health-care costs over the long term," says Jim Younker, general manager of COP. "In providing access to our unique programs and facilities, WinSport is fully focused on developing more Olympic champions — role models and heroes whose international success will ultimately drive more Albertans to increased physical activities."

Meanwhile, Canada's federal government pays lip service to the problem. "Sport Canada has several goals, but I guess the predominant one is to contribute to the life of Canadians," said Stephen Owen, then the minister of Sport, moments before the start of the Athens Olympics. "And I think if, at the end of the day, we didn't win a medal but we found that the level of health and physical activity in Canadian culture was increased, that would be a really good thing."

Two years later, Owen's successor, Michael Chong, declared that "high-performance sport is only one side of the equation. Equally important is broad-based community sport and physical fitness, sports like soccer, rugby, softball and activities such as swimming, dance and jogging." Chong reiterated the importance of sport participation a few months later. "One of the areas that needs to be addressed is increased participation for Canadians in general. We are currently looking at various ways and public policy initiatives that we can undertake that would allow us to increase participation."

Fixing the infrastructure

Canadians agree but are waiting for someone to take action. In 2006, provincial ministers responsible for sport estimated that over $15 billion would be needed to repair and upgrade all public recreational facilities in Canada. They went on to add that there hasn't been a comprehensive program dedicated to the construction of sports facilities since 1967. These figures are not lost on Pat Fiacco, the mayor of Regina, who says, "There is a sport infrastructure gap that has left all too many communities badly in need of new sports facilities and struggling to maintain older, worn-out facilities."

Ontario minister Jim Watson says that 30 to 50 percent of the province's sport structures are at the end of their useful life. The situation is particularly dire in Toronto, Canada's most populous city. It has only two Olympic-sized swimming pools and one of them leaks. Facilities for unique sports such as cycling don't exist. Karen Pitre, chair of Toronto Sports Council, notes, "The need for sport infrastructure is desperate. There's nothing here."

Things aren't much better on the prairies. In Manitoba, amateur sports groups (especially indoor soccer players) are clamouring for more field space, saying they're sick of practising in sub-par school gyms at ungodly hours of the morning or night.

The friendly confines of WinSport notwithstanding, there is a significant sport infrastructure gap in Calgary. Todd Simonson, director of officiating with Calgary Minor Basketball, says space is the biggest problem facing his sport in the Stampede City. This comment is supported by the fact that during the 2007 municipal election, candidates fighting for the position of mayor noted that the last year a recreation facility was built in the city was 1982. Calgarians continue to wait.

Jim Watson, Ontario minister of sport and promotion, said in an interview, "Where will these kids get active?" Canada's failing sport infrastructure system has an impact not only on the activity levels of all Canadians, but also on the country's ability to produce elite athletes. Dr. Bruce Kidd, an Olympian at the 1964 Olympics, notes that elite athletes need first-class facilities if they are to develop their talents. "There's no surprise why we are not on the podium as often as we should be," Watson says. "We just don't have the facilities."

Creating a sport culture

According to the University of Alberta's Marvin Washington, sport infrastructure funding is only half of the equation in developing a summer sport culture in Canada. The other half rests in developing a sporting environment that allows kids to fulfill their dreams in summer sporting activities.

Washington notes that in the United States soccer is the number-one sport in terms of participation, but basketball and football are king. This is explained by the fact that kids in the U.S. dream of playing in the National Basketball Association or National Football League. Kids don't dream of playing professional soccer because, until recently, professional soccer leagues didn't exist in the country.

As for Canada, participation in basketball is at an all-time high, but kids don't dream of playing collegiate basketball or football. They dream of playing in the National Hockey League. Kevin Tyler, former head of the University of Alberta's Canadian Athletic Coaching Centre and a Olympian in bobsledding, agrees. In an interview with a University of Alberta newspaper, he said that "kids get involved in sport for a reason — there has to be a goal to work towards. Why are millions of kids playing hockey? Even if we have millions of kids who are delusional about making the NHL, those are millions of kids who are getting fit. And every one dollar spent in fitness results in four dollars in health-care savings. We have a population in trouble, so at the very least we have healthier people."

However, with a sport infrastructure gap that fails in providing Canadians with the facilities they need, Canada's youth not only aren't getting fit, they also are not developing their skills to compete at the Olympics. And Washington doesn't see this changing any time soon. "Before you have high-performing athletes, you need development ... it is hard to develop high-performance summer athletes if you don't have the facilities." Facilities do exist on the winter side of things. When asked why Canada's winter athletes are succeeding on the international circuit, he reiterates that it's because "the development system in Canada is focused on winter sport."

How do we make it happen on the summer side of sport as well?

In January 2009, the federal government provided evidence that it was prepared to start answering that very question by contributing $500 million through a matching grant program to assist in the repairs of sport facilities across Canada.

The remaining part of that answer was offered in a letter to George Gross of the *Toronto Sun* from Paul Henderson, a high-ranking International Olympic Committee member and past president of the International Sailing Federation. Henderson wrote that athletic facilities with a significant economic impact can tap into the $8.8 billion earmarked under the Government of Canada's infrastructure program, the Building Canada Fund (BCF).

Statistics released by Sask Sport indicate that amateur sport events in communities throughout Saskatchewan have a significant impact on the economy. The organization's estimate was that from 2000 to 2007, national and international sporting events helped contribute over $147 million to the local economy. And this figure didn't take into account the tens of millions spent on local sporting events that communities host each year. The report went on to conclude that sport is a significant contributor to the economic well-being of communities.

As continuing efforts are made to educate the government about the economic importance of sport throughout Canada, sport can be a major benefactor of BCF. It is through BCF that all levels of government — provincial, municipal, and federal — can find a way to invest $10 billion over the next ten years to repair athletic facilities across the country.

But this isn't the whole story. Washington notes that a lack of infrastructure is not the only reason that summer sports are failing to produce athletes. Another reason is that there aren't enough development opportunities within football, basketball, and soccer. Canada has to change this and it begins with Canada's universities. "Sport at the university level needs to be reborn," says famed Olympic broadcaster Brian Williams. This is where the Road to

Excellence program and its $72 million in sport funding can make an impact.

As of January 2007, more than two thousand of Canada's best collegiate athletes were in the United States on athletic scholarships. More has to be done to keep our athletes in Canada. Bob Phillip, athletic director of the University of British Columbia, says, "We see so many athletes going to the States every year that we felt Canadian schools should be doing more to try and offer opportunities for Canadian students to play in Canada."

Washington says we can retain our best athletes here at home by enhancing the Canadian collegiate experience. The NCAA sixty-four-team basketball tournament galvanizes the American and Canadian public over a three-week period every spring. There's no reason why Canada couldn't create something similar with funding from the Road to Excellence program. An American-style tournament would put pressure on coaches and athletes to perform and give kids a dream to build upon. "Over time, Canadian kids may realize that Canadian colleges can compete with U.S. schools," he notes.

Athletes are also driven to the United States by financial incentives available to them there. A full-ride scholarship worth tens of thousands of dollars to a prestigious American school is often the deciding point. Canadian universities need "to provide athletes with larger scholarships or incentives to keep the better Canadian athletes from leaving or going down south for school," says student athlete Rob Cooper.

Marek Glowacki, former coach of the University of Alberta track and field team, says, "Almost every student athlete I know is going to school, training, and holding down a full time job at the same time. If they had better financial support, if they had money for food, accommodation, and tuition, then it would be a different story. They could focus on academics and training and they could be really producing good results in both areas."

In Canada, scholarships are available to student athletes to help defer the cost of tuition. Canadian scholarship rules, however, unlike those in the U.S., prohibit institutions from paying for room, board, and books. That isn't to suggest that other programs, like Road to Excellence, couldn't fund these costs directly. Armed with $72 million, the RTE plan can assist our universities in keeping student athletes in Canada.

Washington is quick to point out that kids in the United States dream of playing college football or basketball at Duke, Stanford, Michigan, or UCLA. There is no reason to suggest that kids here in Canada couldn't someday aspire to play basketball, football, volleyball, or soccer at the universities of Calgary, Toronto, or Manitoba. And when that begins to happen, Canada will be close to implementing a culture of sport ... that is, summer sport.

11

One-Stop Shopping: Implementing Excellence

Tracy's Olympic dream had been over thirty years in the making, but 2007 was the start of making her dream a reality. The top eight boats in the lightweight women's double at the 2007 World Rowing Championships in Munich, Germany, would automatically be given entry to the 2008 Olympic Games. Anything less than a top-eight finish would mean having to race in an Olympic qualifier mere months before the start of the Beijing Olympics, and that was the last thing she wanted.

With the importance of the 2007 rowing season weighing on her, Tracy knew that getting practice time in a double with a new rowing partner was absolutely critical. For the third time in three years, she was looking at reformatting her rowing stroke to match that of a new partner.

This time it was twenty-five-year-old Lindsay Jennerich, who had international racing experience as part of Canada's program for athletes under the age of twenty-three, but she had never raced on the senior circuit.

However, despite her youth, Lindsay was having a career year in 2007, proving to Tracy and the coaching staff alike that she was Canada's second-fastest lightweight rower. Top billing still belonged to Tracy.

As they practised together, progress came quickly for the two of them. By June 2007, their speed had improved dramatically. Hopes were high heading into the world cup circuit. In the months that followed, third- and second-place performances at world cups in Linz, Austria, and Lucerne, Switzerland, proved that the two were on course in their drive to the world championships.

World cup and world championship medals are nice, but the Olympic Games, being the focus for most countries, are a whole different animal.

At the 2007 world championships in Munich, with a berth at the Olympic Games on the line, competition hit a fever pitch. Every country raised their game. The 2000-metre races were decided by mere hundredths of a second, world champions were struggling to make the finals, and Tracy was fighting for her Olympic life.

After seven days of racing, Tracy and Lindsay found themselves in the B final of the lightweight women's double. This was unfamiliar territory for Tracy. It was the first time in her international rowing career that she wasn't racing for a medal on the final day of competition. What she was racing for, instead, was an Olympic berth. The top two boats in the B final would have a ticket to the Olympics and everyone else would have to wait for another chance.

With 500 metres to go, Tracy and Lindsay were in second. But all that was separating the top three boats was a mere six-tenths of a second. The race was virtually deadlocked. Focusing inward, the women put their heads down and raced as hard as they could to the finish line. Beep, Beep, Beep. It was a photo finish. No one had any idea where they had finished until the results were displayed on the huge electronic board mounted above the spectator stands.

Tracy glanced at the board. Canada had finished first. She was going to the Olympics.

≈

"You can't beat the Aussies in swimming and you can't beat the Americans in track and field," says Jim Byers of the *Toronto Star*. His comment was seconded by former Olympic track and field coach Ron Bowker, who feels that track and field isn't part of our culture the way it is in Kenya and other African nations, making it difficult for Canadians to compete.

However, people told Ken Read the same thing following the 2002 Winter Olympics in Salt Lake City. "Canadians can't compete against the Austrians in downhill skiing," they said. At the time, Canada had its worst-ever Olympics in alpine skiing. But looking at the same team now, Canada won a record number of medals on the world cup circuit in 2007-2008 and almost bettered it in 2009.

Stephen Brunt, a writer with the *Globe and Mail*, figures that loads of dough and a rearrangement of societal and fiscal priorities are what's required to put Canada's summer athletes over the top at the Olympics.

But don't tell that to Mike Spracklen, head coach of the Canadian men's rowing team, or Anne Merklinger, CEO of CanoeKayak Canada. Spracklen took over the men's rowing program in 2001 following a disastrous Olympic Games in Sydney, in which only one Canadian man (Derek Porter) rowed in an Olympic final. Since then, Spracklen's boys have won four world championships and three Olympic medals, one of which was gold. As a result of Spracklen's leadership, Canada's men's rowing program has become the most dominant program in the world.

Merklinger helped resurrect a sports program that had limited funding and won a single Olympic medal from 1988 to 1996. Since then, CanoeKayak Canada has won eight medals at the past three Summer Olympiads. And in Adam van Koeverden and Caroline Brunet, the organization has produced two of Canada's most decorated Olympians. "The key is leadership," says Jim Christie of the *Globe and Mail*.

"Dammit, let's do things right!"

These were the words Ken Read uttered when he took over as Alpine Canada president in 2002. Since then the organization has done just that: increasing corporate sponsorship tenfold, strengthening Canada's domestic program by getting Canada's best to race head-to-head more often, and improving Canada's international ranking from twelfth to fifth in the FIS World Cup standings. Canada's ski team was the youngest of all the competing countries in Torino, and while no Canadian skier made the podium, two missed a medal by less than 0.2 of a second.

"Ken totally changed it," says track star Donovan Bailey. "He has the connections to get sponsorship dollars. As a former athlete he knows what it takes to produce winners."

As Alpine Canada moves toward 2010, the goals remain the same. "The number-one goal is to make sure that we have the resources and are delivering these resources to our top team to ensure that they are able to perform," says Read. "Our second goal is to continue building the athlete development system." It appears to be working. The results from the 2007 and 2008 seasons prove that Canada will be a force in 2010.

"In the 1990s, as the public sector cut funding, we didn't waiver from our focus," says Merklinger in explaining the success of CanoeKayak Canada at the past three Olympiads. "We resisted temptation to expand our administration and focused as many resources as possible on our athletes and coaches."

Today, seven coaches work with the Canadian national team while regional coaches have been hired to identify and train paddlers across the country.

Merklinger has developed coaching education programs for her coaches and has appointed as head of the domestic system a former Olympian who interacts with clubs across the country. As she explains, "It is important for us to provide opportunities to our coaches."

The benefactor is the sport itself. Not only is canoe-kayak Canada's most successful sport at the past three Summer Olympiads, but as Merklinger herself acknowledges, "Athletes in competitive programs have increased by twenty, or twenty-five percent. In 2003, we had forty-five clubs. Now, we have eighty. Twenty-five (of those clubs) have full-time year-round coaches. There are a lot of opportunities to be a professional canoeist and kayaker."

"Friends come and go, but gold medals last forever," were the first words Spracklen uttered to his troops back in 2001. Proud of his relatively small group of athletes, Spracklen came to Rowing Canada with one purpose alone: to win gold.

Training out of a building condemned for demolition, Spracklen built his program from the ground up on one tried and trusted trait: hard work. Relying on the principle that the harder a person works, the more their body adjusts to the work, Spracklen squeezes every last drop of energy out of his athletes each and every day. For some, including many of Canada's sport physiologists, it is too much, but those who compete for the man believe in him and his refinements.

"There's no magic in it," says athlete Jake Wetzel. "The whole time he puts us out of our comfort zone. You're rewarded for failure, for pushing to the point where you fall apart. You're not rewarded for mediocrity."

And so they keep pushing. A self-obsessed rowing fan, Spracklen monitors every one of his twenty-plus weekly training sessions, ensuring that his athletes are piling up the mileage so that even on their worst day the team can walk away with the gold.

Merklinger, like Read and Spracklen, is proof positive that Canadians can compete with the rest of the world. But doing so requires planning and preparation. It requires people who are knowledgeable about sport and know how to put that knowledge to use. It requires people who understand that the job of a sports organization is to invest in opportunities for its athletes. It requires people who are passionate about sport.

Spracklen and Merklinger answer to this description. So does Alpine Canada, which is why it pulls in $13 million from corporate sponsors like Pontiac GMC, Bombardier, Loblaw Companies, WestJet, and Telus. Meanwhile, sports like cycling and boxing rely on government handouts.

Unfortunately, stories of success in Canada's summer sport organizations have been the exception in the twenty-first century. Three-time Olympic gold medallist Marnie McBean agrees, noting that "when Canadian athletes do well, it's the exception — they survive despite the system."

From fragmentation to unity

After winning two gold medals at the 1984 Olympics, Alex Baumann sought work within Canada's amateur sport system but was quietly shown the door everywhere he went. Frustrated with a sporting system that failed to be held accountable for its actions, he wrote a scathing article in a Quebec newspaper on Canada's then-floundering swim program. Ostracized for speaking the truth, he left for Australia to pursue a graduate degree at the University of Queensland, eventually becoming manager of sport programs with the Queensland Academy of Sport. He then held various positions with the Queensland government before becoming CEO of Queensland Swimming in 1999. Some three years later, Baumann was promoted to the position of director of the Queensland Academy of Sport, overseeing 650 athletes across twenty-one different sports. Installing a personal philosophy that he describes as "athlete-centred, coach driven, service supported, but performance based," Baumann had his Queensland athletes thriving on the international scene.

The Athens Olympics were the most successful in the academy's history, with Queensland athletes winning seventeen of Australia's forty-nine medals.

Some five years after those Athens Games, Baumann, as executive director of Canada's Road to Excellence program, is hoping to duplicate his successes for Australia by creating a similar system here in Canada. But the challenges are daunting. He acknowledged as much in an interview with the Halifax *Chronicle*, saying, "An integrated system that gives coaches and athletes of all levels access to similar support services and development opportunities does not exist for Canada's summer athletes."

He's right. Canada's summer sport organizations are spread across the country, with Victoria home to Canada's rowing team, Halifax home to Canada's canoe-kayak team, and every other summer sport organization somewhere in between. "Right now what we have are isolated pockets of excellence," notes Alex Gardiner.

Sherraine Schalm, who made history in 2005 by becoming the first-ever Canadian woman to win a medal at the world fencing championships, notes that winter athletes are lucky because they have a training institute in Canada — virtually all of Canada's winter athletes train in a centralized location, managed by WinSport Canada — while summer athletes go all over the country.

Martha Henderson, an Olympian at the 2008 Games in the sport of sailing, agrees, saying that summer athletes are fragmented across the country.

And many of the facilities themselves aren't conducive to producing high-performing athletes. For example, Canada's rowers train in Victoria out of a boathouse that lacks many of the modern amenities that today's athletes require, such as weight rooms, sport therapists, and doctors. Barney Williams, a silver medallist in the sport of rowing at the 2004 Olympics, explained in an article published by the *Toronto Star* that rowers in Victoria must avoid water skiers and fisherman on Elk Lake during their on-the-water training sessions and then make their way to separate venues for weight training, food, and treatment. "This reduces recovery time between training sessions, time which is arguably just as important as the training itself," he said.

And yet, Canada's rowers are lucky in comparison with many summer sport athletes. Unlike rowing, many of Canada' summer sport organizations don't offer a centralized training centre for their athletes. Canada's best boxers are scattered across the continent, as are many of Canada's, cyclists, fencers, sailors, wrestlers, shooters, and weightlifters. These athletes train in makeshift facilities with a lack of amenities that our winter athletes enjoy. This negligence puts our summer athletes at a serious disadvantage internationally.

Pierre Lafontaine, the CEO of Swimming Canada, claims that "the idea of a central training centre is important because it gives kids who train in small towns across Canada, like Moose Jaw or Prince George, access to infrastructure that their local club might not offer." Lafontaine remarked in a radio interview with *Swimming World* that while careful to protect the "club environment," a centralized swimming centre creates an environment where world-class swimming is talked about every day.

Lafontaine has helped produce just such an environment in his quest to rebuild Swimming Canada. Today the organization offers two stand-alone centres where kids are given first-class coaching in a high-performance environment while enabling them to retain their allegiance to their home club. The experiment seems to be working, with Swimming Canada winning its first Olympic medal in over eight years at the 2008 Beijing Games.

But the fact remains that Canada's summer sport organizations aren't providing their athletes with the level of services that winter organizations give their athletes. Baumann, CEO of the Road to Excellence program, says, "I think we need to take a look at where are all the resources are going and make informed decisions in terms of, is this the best use of the funds to get the results we want?"

Adham Sharara, president of the International Table Tennis Federation, is one such Canadian who has taken a look at where our resources are going. He notes that an integrated type of sport system doesn't exist in Canada. "The problem in Canada's summer sport system is there is no unity. We are a sport system that is completely divided, with everyone in their own corner. What we have to do is pool our resources, create efficient plans, and ensure opportunities for all Canadians."

Documents released by Sport Canada bear out Sharara's comments, showing that in 2006 Sport Canada provided funding assistance to both the Coaches of Canada, who represent the profession of coaching, and the Coaching Association of Canada, whose mandate is to improve the profession of coaching. In 2006, sport funding was provided to True Sport, which promotes the life skills derived from sport; Participaction, which promotes participation in sport; and the Canadian Association for Health, Physical Education, Recreation, and Dance, which promotes the healthy development of children in sport. The list goes on to name more than fifty sport organizations, each with their own office and staff who receive some form of government assistance.

This duplication of resources helps explain why the resources are not getting to coaching and programs.

Taking coaching seriously

While we're on the topic of coaching, consider this statement about the Athens Games by Mark Lowry, then the executive director of the COC: "We have a coaching situation that is deplorable, unacceptable."

In a 2009 report to the Minister of State for Sport, the Coaching Association of Canada noted that there is a shortage of candidates for high-performance coaching positions.

Russ Anber, a boxing analyst on TSN, notes that we don't take coaching seriously in Canada. "Coaching is a legitimate profession, supporting the development of hundreds of athletes, but if your son or daughter came to you saying that they'd want to be a coach, you'd have to tell them good luck ... Coaching in Canada has become sort of a benevolent position where father or mother helps out to coach the local school team." Anber adds that "there is no formal way to become a full-time professional coach in Canada."

And those fortunate enough to coach full-time seem to lack accountability for their performance, holding onto their positions year after year. Donovan Bailey, Olympic gold medallist in 1996, notes that coaches within Canada's amateur sports system "ultimately never blame themselves."

Tom Ponting, the only Canadian swimmer to have won Olympic medals in three separate Olympiads, feels that the philosophy of Canadian coaches is to not get fired. "Coaches in Canada are retained for having never done anything wrong, but often they haven't done anything right either," he says.

Pierre Lafontaine, the newly appointed CEO of Swimming Canada, acknowledged moments before the start of the 2005 World Aquatic Championships that "coaches have to start being accountable for their performance." Two years later, he said, "Sport organizations are often the last refuge of the incompetent."

Mark Greenwald, then the director of the Olympic Oval, notes that in Canada "there are too many people in sport leadership positions who are not taking responsibility for their performance ... In the United States these people are fired."

Not so in Canada. At the 2007 U20 World Cup of Soccer, Canada's team failed to score a single goal. But that didn't stop the coach of that team, Dale Mitchell, from being promoted to the position of head coach of Canada's senior men's soccer team. With Mitchell at the helm, Canada's senior men's program was a flop as it tried to qualify for the 2010 World Cup in South Africa. Rick Brennan quit the team and said he would "never again play under Mitchell."

Dwayne De Rosario said he could not understand "why a man who coached the Under-20s to a miserable no goals in their world cup could have been given the men's job." In October 2008 the men's soccer program was put out of its misery when it was eliminated from world cup qualifying. In March 2009 the Canadian Soccer Association cut ties with Mitchell, but the cash-strapped organization will have to continue to pay him up to 2010, when his contract expires.

Alex Gardiner, the then senior director of programming with the COC, acknowledges that there has to be more professionalism in Canada's sports system. Pat Fiacco, the mayor of Regina and a high-ranking official in boxing, feels that Canada's amateur sports system has to be managed like a business. Never has this been more apparent. With the inherent duplication of resources, a lack of accountability within the coaching ranks, and a lack of professionalism among Canada's sporting organizations, changes need to be made.

Sherraine Schalm, Canada's first-ever medallist at the fencing world championships, recommends the creation of a sports institute. "Training centres are the only way to succeed," she says. Joshua Riker-Fox, a bronze medallist at the 2007 Pan American Games in the modern pentathlon, recommends that such an institute be modelled after the one in Australia.

And Adham Sharara, president of the International Table Tennis Federation, recommends the creation of a central sports institute. Daniel Igali, Olympic gold medallist in the sport of wrestling at the 2000 Olympics, says such an institute would "greatly assist summer sports in Canada."

Canada needs a place where all of its summer sporting bodies operate out of the same location. Much like their winter counterparts, summer athletes need a place where the resources they require to succeed are at their disposal. Canada's coaches need a place where they can learn and develop state-of-the-art methodologies. Canada needs a place where camps, massage, nutritionists, psychologists, regeneration facilities, and room and board are provided free of charge. A place where Canada's brightest minds are brought together to share ideas. A place where synergies are created through free-flowing communication within and between the various sporting bodies.

No lack of opportunity

As Canada's summer athletes jealously watch their winter counterparts train in state-of-the-art facilities in Calgary, they may not realize that Canada has had an opportunity to create a similar institute on the summer side. Since 1976, Canada has hosted an Olympic Games, two Commonwealth Games, a Pan American Games, a Universaide Games, countless world championships, and numerous Canada Games. However, because of a lack of foresight on behalf of the organizers and a lack of resources, none of these events has been leveraged to bring Canada's summer sports organizations together and do what WinSport has done for winter sports.

Frank King, president of the Calgary Organizing Committee for the 1988 Winter Olympics, recognized in the lead-up to the Calgary Olympics that it wasn't enough to have world-class facilities. They also needed the right people to run them. King says the organizers asked themselves, "Who's going to run the facilities after the Games?" The answer to that question was CODA. "CODA (now WinSport) created the baby," says King, adding that the vision of the 1988 organizing committee was to create a legacy in Calgary. "We didn't want a sixteen-day circus if all we were left with at the end was a big patch of brown grass."

For one reason or another, those organizing other international multi-sport events in Canada have not applied this vision. "The Victoria Games (the 1994 Commonwealth Games) were an excellent Games, but afterwards everyone went their own way," says King. The same thing applies to the 2005 World Aquatic Championships in Montreal. The event was well received by the Montreal community and was attended by athletes from around the globe. Unfortunately, all that was left after the event were three outdoor pools that no one in the swimming community will dare use during the winter months.

According to King, this lack of vision exists largely because of a lack of leadership. "We don't seem to have the same leadership in summer sports; we can't seem to get things together ... but if ever there was a model on how to do it, all (the summer sports) would need is to look at how our winter sports program did it."

So let's do just that.

The payoff for Calgary

At the 1988 Games in Calgary, just as at the 1976 Games in Montreal, the Canadian team failed to win gold. But unlike the Montreal Games, the Calgary Games made money. And that was largely a result of what happened in Los Angeles.

The 1984 Los Angeles Games were the first exhibition of strategic sports sponsorship. Although the number of sponsors had grown for the Olympic Games, it was not until the L.A. Games in 1984 that the great potential value of sporting mega-events became clear to the IOC. Success did not lie in bringing together a growing number of sponsors; exactly the opposite: reducing the number of sponsors while increasing the amount each sponsor paid. The organizers limited the number of sponsors to thirty-five and set out specific conditions regarding exclusivity. A list of commercial sectors was drawn up, and only one representative could sponsor each sector. Selected companies were willing to pay larger amounts since they were guaranteed exclusivity, which had a major effect on U.S. and international television audiences. As a result, the Games became a guaranteed economic success.

However, the marketing of the Olympic Games in Los Angeles was limited to the host country and U.S companies. Following those Games, and building on the L.A. model, the International Olympic Committee designed the Olympic global sponsorship program known as The Olympic Partners (TOP). TOP sold companies the right to use Olympic symbols worldwide in return for a significant fee. Under IOC supervision, the Calgary 1988 Winter Games saw the implementation of the first TOP program. The result was an economic windfall for Calgary. What's more, television revenues reached a peak at the same time. "The largest jump in television revenues occurred before Calgary in 1988," says Kevin Wamsley, director of the Olympic Studies Centre.

In an article written for the CBC, Tara Kimura reports that "television rights for the Calgary Games increased by over $220 million from the 1984 Winter Games, a near 200 percent increase in only four years." Bob Barney, founding director of the International Centre for Olympic studies, explains that Calgary benefited uniquely because of a bidding war between the three American networks vying for exclusive broadcast rights.

Seeking to re-establish itself as the Olympic network, ABC saw tremendous advertising opportunities with the Calgary Games. Thanks to the Games being in the Mountain Time Zone, the events fit nicely into prime time programming in the U.S. When everything was said and done, ABC paid $398 million for the Games — nearly $40 million more than what was paid for the 1992 Games in Albertville, France.

From the early days of Calgary's Winter Olympic Games bid, the vision of the Calgary Organizing Committee was to establish a post-Olympic legacy with future Canadian athletes in mind. Using an unprecedented $150-million surplus, organizers created an endowment following the Games to preserve the facilities from the 1988 Olympics, which CODA — and later WinSport — was given the responsibility to manage. On July 20, 1988, the ownership of Canada Olympic Park was transferred from the federal government to CODA for the nominal cost of one dollar. Furthermore, two separate endowments from the Calgary Organizing Committee and the federal government totalling over $65 million ensured that the facilities of the 1988 Games would provide ongoing benefits to the Canadian sports community.

As a result, Calgary is the hub of Canada's winter sports movement. WinSport's offices are located at Canada Olympic Park, allowing the leaders of WinSport to communicate with Canada's winter athletes on an almost daily basis. WinSport's main goal is to house all fifteen of Canada's winter sport organizations, as well as the leaders who oversee them, in Calgary. Dr. Roger Jackson, who oversees the OTP program, works in an office building operated by WinSport at Canada Olympic Park.

The result is a winter sport movement that has streamlined the use of resources and is managing them in an efficient manner.

Will Vancouver learn from Calgary?

With the 2010 Winter Games in Vancouver on the horizon, some are concerned that Calgary and WinSport may play less of an impact in the years to come. Gordon Ritchie, chairman of WinSport from 2008 to 2010, quickly dispels this notion, saying that Calgary and WinSport will remain Canada's winter sport hub following the 2010 Games. This provides hope to Canada's summer athletes.

With its moderate oceanic climate and its state-of-the-art athletic facilities from the 2010 Games, Vancouver would be well-positioned to become Canada's next summer sporting institute — something that Chris Rudge of the COC says is already in the works. It is hoped that the Vancouver Olympic Organizing Committee can create the type of surpluses enjoyed by those organizing the 1988 Winter Olympics. This is definitely possible. NBC is paying $820 million for the right to broadcast the 2010 Games, a 33 percent increase from what it paid to broadcast the 2006 Games in Torino. And the domestic sponsorship revenue target is $760 million.

Canada's summer athletes can only hope that the Vancouver Organizing Committee has the same vision as those who organized the Calgary Games. With the creation of an endowment to preserve the facilities from the Games and a recognition that someone has to manage the facilities after the Games, there is little doubt that the 2010 winter facilities could be transformed to satisfy the needs of our summer athletes.

The speed skating oval could be transformed into Canada's first fully functional 400m indoor running track, complete with gymnasiums, weight rooms, offices, and regeneration rooms. A short five-minute drive from the oval is the newly constructed John Leckey Boathouse, home to the University of British Columbia rowing team and fully functional for Canada's kayakers, canoeists, and runners. Vancouver is already home to Canada's national swim team. There is little question that the newly constructed sport centre on the UBC campus could be transformed to house Canada's national basketball, volleyball, field hockey, and gymnastic teams. With the proper vision, Vancouver could become Canada's next sporting institute for summer sports.

Another key to summer success is coaching. Summer athletes require a stable of professional coaches: coaches who are knowledgeable and experienced, who have the same desire to win as the athletes themselves. And winning should be the basis on which they are judged.

Similar to the situation in which Speed Skating Canada is a client of the Olympic Oval in Calgary, national sport programs involved with the newly proposed summer institute should become clients of the institute. Each of the respective sport programs would pay the institute to use their coaches, facilities, and services, with the purpose of facilitating development. This type of system should be fully integrated and predicated on performance, creating an atmosphere in which athletes are accountable to their coaches; the coaches are accountable to the institute; the institute is accountable to the national sport programs; and the national sport programs are accountable to their funding partner, the independent sports commission. This idea would bring to fruition what Alex Baumann describes as an athlete-focused, coach-driven, service-supported, but performance-based system: a system where the institute provides the services, coaches choose the services they want, and the athletes benefit.

PART FOUR

Putting the Plan into Action

12

The End of Spectator Sports: Getting Canadian Athletes into the Games

Tracy was a competitor. She would race anyone at any time. It didn't matter where or with whom — on land or on the water, man or woman, young or old — if someone was willing, she was ready. And while winning wasn't always the outcome, it was always what drove her.

Winning had come easily to her. She was a world champion and for the past two seasons hadn't lost a race of any significance in Canada. By the fall of 2007, however, she wasn't winning with her usual regularity. She was coming off a disappointing seventh-place finish at the 2007 world championships and was no longer the fastest lightweight woman in Canada. That distinction belonged to Melanie Kok, a twenty-five-year-old from St. Catharines, Ontario. Melanie's arrival meant a change in Canada's lightweight double boat. Tracy would still have her seat, but Lindsay Jennerich was out.

Faced with the reality of having to row a double with her fourth partner in as many years, Tracy began challenging the system itself. She had lost confidence in her coach, Laryssa Biesenthal. Biesenthal was a relative novice to the coaching ranks, and Tracy doubted that she had the ability to get Melanie and her onto the podium at the Olympics. So she demanded a change. She wanted to row with men's coach Mike Spracklen. Spracklen was a legend in Canadian rowing. He had coached Canadian men's crews to gold at the 2002, 2003, and 2007 world championships. He had coached crews to at least one medal at four consecutive Olympiads. Despite being overburdened with preparation of his own crews for the Olympic Games in Beijing, Mike welcomed the two women into his program. He vowed that he would give them the attention and resources they needed.

Rowing Canada, meanwhile, had other ideas. They put Tracy under strict orders not to train with Mike. He was the men's coach, not the lightweight women's coach. Tracy and Melanie, according to Rowing Canada, were to return to their former coach. The two parties were at loggerheads. Sporting officials were flown in from across the country to convince the two to accept Rowing Canada's decision.

Then, at the eleventh hour, a compromise was reached. Tracy and Melanie were to move to London, Ontario, and train under coach Al Morrow, international rowing coach of the year in 1999 and a member of Canada's Sports Hall of Fame.

Morrow understood rowing like Scotty Bowman understood hockey. He was experienced; he had attended each and every Olympic Games since 1984; he had the time; he oversaw the under-twenty-three develop-ment team for Rowing Canada and wasn't formally preparing athletes for the 2008 Olympic Games. And he was successful: Canadian crews had won more Olympic medals under his stewardship than under any other coach in the sport. Tracy knew he had the ability to get the results she and Melanie desired.

However, though she and Melanie agreed to the change, one problem remained: London, Ontario, Morrow's hometown, was covered with ice until early April.

∿

Academy-Award-winning actor Robin Williams has been quoted as saying, "Many of my favorite Olympic memories were not gold-medal situations. They were inspiring moments of humanity that transcended borders, obstacles, and languages — and unified people around the world. This unique element is the intersection of sport and the human spirit that are captured in the stories of these athletes regardless of where they have come from." What makes the Olympic Games different from every other athletic competition is that the memories we take from them focus more on the stories of individual athletes than on the country's overall medal count.

Memories of Elizabeth Manley, for example. At the 1988 Olympics, in a figure-skating event that was to be dominated by her rivals Debi Thomas (USA) and Katerina Witt (East Germany), Manley defied the odds by skating the performance of her life, winning not only a silver medal but also the hearts of all Canadians.

And Daniel Igali. As one of twenty-one children in his family in Nigeria, Igali defected to Canada in 1994 following the Commonwealth Games in Victoria because of political unrest in his home country. Six years later we watched as he won Olympic Gold for his new country and proceeded to celebrate by dancing around a Canadian flag on the wrestling mat.

And, outside the Canadian sphere, Robina Muqimyar, a sprinter from war-torn Afghanistan, who in 2004 became the first of two Afghan women to ever compete in an Olympic Games. Muqimyar failed to advance from her heat, but sent a message to the world that her country's women would not be held back any longer.

Arbitrary standards

The marquee event of the 2004 Athens Games was the men's and women's marathon, because it commemorated the origin of the event itself in the country of its origin, Greece. The marathon course covered the legendary route of Phidippides, the Greek soldier who in 490 B.C. ran from Marathon to Athens to bring news of a military victory before dying. During the 2004 race, a Brazilian named Vanderlei de Lima created memories for all who watched. Not only did he win the bronze medal, but he also received the Pierre de Coubertin medal in recognition of his Olympic spirit after being attacked on the racecourse by a spectator. "The Olympic spirit prevailed here," de Lima said. "My determination prevailed."

Unfortunately, no Canadian ran in either the men's or women's marathon that year. Not because they hadn't qualified for the Olympics — in fact, quite the opposite: Olympic organizers had sent out a special request to each participating country to field a full marathon team. The reason Canadians didn't participate was that Canadian officials set their own qualifying standard above the Olympic standard.

For the women's marathon, Canada's qualifying mark was a full nine minutes faster than the Olympic standard and twenty-four seconds faster than Canada's national record. As a result, Nicole Stevenson, Canada's best woman marathoner, did not go to Athens. Meanwhile, the USA's Deena Kastor, who ended up winning a bronze medal in Athens, didn't break Canada's qualifying mark, in 2004, until the Olympic Games themselves.

But athletes in the marathon weren't the only ones being subjected to Canada's strict qualifying standards. In fact, forty-seven of Canada's top athletes weren't in Athens, despite meeting the Olympic qualification standard for their respective sport.

And some didn't go because of technicalities associated with the stringent standard. Jessica Zelinka of Calgary, who won the heptathlon at the Canadian track and field trials in Victoria and followed that performance by breaking Canada's qualifying standard for this event at a meet in Europe, was not in Athens. Zelinka discovered that one of the seven events was wind-aided the day she broke Canada's qualifying standard. Unfortunately, Canadian sport officials were unwilling to look beyond that result, despite evidence indicating that she was able to compete at the Olympic level.

Or how about Audrey Lacroix? Lacroix competed for a spot on the 4x100m medley relay swim team at the 2004 Olympic trials in Montreal. In that relay, four individuals combine to make a team, with each swimmer using a different swimming stroke: freestyle, backstroke, breaststroke, or butterfly. In selecting the best team, most countries select their fastest swimmer over

100m in each of the disciplines. Not Canada. Canada's fastest swimmer in the 100m-butterfly event, Audrey Lacroix, failed to break the COC standard for that stroke and was omitted from the relay team. Jennifer Fratesi was chosen to swim this portion of the relay at the Games, where she finished sixth in the event, well behind Lacroix's time at Canada's aquatic team trials. She was chosen because she qualified for the Games in an unrelated event — the 200m backstroke — and was therefore deemed eligible to swim the butterfly. Canada's medley relay team failed to make it out of their heat at the 2004 Olympics.

Lacroix finished fifth at the 2007 World Aquatic Championships in the 200m butterfly. However, having been denied the experience of competing in Athens, she stumbled in Beijing, failing to advance to the finals.

To represent their country at the Olympics, athletes must first meet the International Olympic Committee's qualifying standard set by each sport's international federation. In addition, IOC member countries, including the Canadian Olympic Committee, may set their own specific qualifying standard. Two years prior to the Olympics in Athens, the COC did just that by changing its qualification standard from a top-sixteen to a top-twelve ranking. This made it more difficult for Canadians than all other international athletes to attend the Games. The COC defended the move, claiming that the more stringent standards motivated athletes to perform and would lead to more medals. But the Athens Games were not only a failure for Canadian athletes, who won a paltry twelve medals, they were also Canada's worst Olympiad since 1972, measuring medals won as a percentage of total available medals. In Athens, Canada won 1.3 percent of the total available medals, compared with 1.5 percent in 2000 and 2.7 percent in 1996.

In an article to Runners Web.com, Bruce Deacon, a two-time Olympian at the 1996 and 2000 Olympic Games but a victim of the top twelve policy, pointed out a discrepancy in the COC's attitude toward athletes. "Canadian Olympic athletes speak to thousands of school children," he wrote. "They bring a positive message that hard work is worthwhile, that dreams are achievable, and that living a healthy lifestyle has great rewards" — values that the COC is quick to promote when lobbying the federal government for public monies. Unfortunately, when the COC leaves the board room and heads for the sporting field, the message changes. COC marketing and communications director Nick Marrone said the Olympics "are about winning. If you don't have a good chance of winning then you shouldn't be there."

"Germany has a top eight standard and does consistently well. We have a top twelve standard," noted COC president Michael Chambers at the Athens Games. However, German athletes like Sebastian Ernst, a track and field athlete, would not have competed in Athens if he were Canadian.

Another argument trotted out by the COC in favour of Canada's restrictive standard in Athens is that future performances by Canadian athletes are not affected by prior Games experience or multiple-Games appearances. Research and common sense suggest otherwise. A study conducted by one of the COC's own directors showed that 75 to 80 percent of athletes who win medals are in their second Games. This makes sense, says VANOC vice president Cathy Priestner Allinger. "As any Olympian who has been to two (Games) will tell you, the first time is not the same as the second — it's a whole new experience."

In 2004, recognizing the merits of prior Games experience, the COC relaxed its qualifying standard for winter athletes from a top sixteen standard to the lesser standard employed by the International Olympic Committee. Why? To help its athletes prepare for Vancouver 2010. "The main reason, the driver behind this, is the fact that Canada is hosting the 2010 Winter Games," says Karen Purdy, chair of the COC Athletes' Council.

Adds Chris Rudge, CEO of the COC, "Canadians may in turn see a handful of fortieth- and fiftieth-place finishes from youngsters there to get their feet wet. Everybody's prepared to live with that. Some have been disappointed in the past but it'll be important that every young athlete understands they may not do as well as they'd hoped; but the experience they glean from it should make them better prepared for 2010."

The end result was Canada's best ever finish at an Olympiad. While some of these younger athletes did come fortieth or fiftieth, as expected, others went on to Olympic glory: athletes such as Chandra Crawford, who was ranked forty-fifth in the world coming into Torino and shocked everyone by winning Olympic Gold in the women's cross-country sprint.

Consistent standards

Recognizing the success of our winter athletes in Torino, many Canadians hoped that a consistent qualification standard for Canadian athletes would be set for all Olympic Games, beginning in Beijing in 2008. That didn't happen. While the coc agreed to relax its stringent top-twelve qualifying standard in Beijing, many of Canada's best Summer Olympians still watched the 2008 Games at home. Two high-profile dressage riders, Cindy Ishoy and Ashley Nicole-Holzer, members of Canada's bronze-medal-winning team in dressage at the 1988 Games in Seoul, bypassed the Beijing Games, saying they couldn't afford to meet the Canadian qualifying criteria. Ishoy noted in a *Globe and Mail* article that the Canadian criteria are so costly, she would have to win Lotto 6/49 just to qualify.

And our Olympic marathoners? In 2008, for the second straight Olympiad, Canada failed to send an athlete in that sport to the Olympics. Canada's Olympic standard for the marathon was more than a full minute faster than what the international power of the sport, Kenya, requires.

Meanwhile, for the 2010 Games, all indications are that Canada will send a full team of winter athletes using the international standards employed by virtually all Olympic nations.

Why do Canada's summer athletes get a raw deal compared with winter athletes? As it turns out, the issue has more to do with money than anything else. The coc's Chris Rudge claims that dollars or resources are not behind the restrictive qualifying standard placed on our summer athletes. But he has also noted to the sport community that if the provinces were to come forward with added resources, Canada's restrictive standard could be reviewed and possibly relaxed. Indeed, with added resources flowing to our winter athletes as they prepare for Vancouver 2010, that has happened.

The Vancouver factor

It is imperative that Canada's winter athletes win in Vancouver in 2010. "The only way that the Vancouver Olympic Games will be considered a success is if Canadian athletes win gold," notes John Furlong, CEO of the Vancouver Olympics.

The 1988 Winter Olympics in Calgary and the 1976 Summer Games in Montreal proved that this is no easy task. But things are different this time around. Sport officials have recognized, for 2010, that if Canada wants to win gold medals, it has to support its athletes. "We have to make it easy for them to play, perform, and train," Furlong says about Canada's winter athletes. This includes making sure "they don't have to worry about having food to eat and that they don't have to worry about coaches and therapists and sport science and medicine and all those things."

Support, however, takes money, and Canada's winter sport programs have an abundance of it heading into 2010. Canada's winter athletes are armed with $55 million in funding from the government of Canada for the Own the Podium program. This is over and above funding from Sport Canada in which organizations like Alpine Canada, Bobsleigh Canada Skeleton, and Speed Skating Canada have seen a 400-percent increase in funding since 2000. An additional $600 million is being spent by the federal government to develop state-of-the-art athletic facilities in Vancouver: facilities Canadian athletes will be given earlier access to than the rest of the world. Then there is an additional $25 million in funding from the government of Canada to promote the 2010 Olympic Torch relay in Canada and a further $900 million needed for Games security.

After the federal tab has been tallied, there is an additional $2 billion in provincial and municipal projects to prepare the city of Vancouver for the Games.

Then there are the Olympic sponsorships. Well-known Canadian companies like Air Canada, Birks, Bay, RBC, Bell, General Motors, Rona, and many others are putting forth nearly $1 billion to be associated with the Vancouver 2010 Games. Money from these sponsorships is going to support Canada's winter athletes. There are also the non-Olympic sponsorship agreements in which companies such as WestJet, Visa, Bombardier, Dow, Sheraton, Husky, Finning, Shaw, Canadian Pacific, and ING are funnelling funds to assist Canada's winter athletes in whatever way they can.

General Motors, as part of its arrangement with Alpine Canada, provides a vehicle for one year to members of the Canadian national Alpine Ski team who win a world cup race, finish on the podium at the world championships, or finish among the top ten in the end-of-season rankings.

Molson Canada, as part of its arrangement with Hockey Canada, presented a $200,000 cheque to help family members of the women's national hockey team attend the Olympics in Italy.

And how about Petro-Canada? Through its Athlete Family Program, it will host and accommodate two immediate family members of all participating Canadian Olympic and Paralympic athletes competing at the 2010 Games.

The list goes on.

"There has been no better time in the last fifty years to be a Canadian winter athlete," notes Furlong. "Sponsors are hiring athletes in jobs tailored to them and corporations are sponsoring them. Many can finally do what top athletes around the world have been allowed to do: train full-time without having to worry about losing a job."

The athletes, in turn, are using the support to their advantage by winning medals — lots of them. Canada's winter athletes won a record 184 medals in world championship and world cup events in 2007-2008 — a trend that has continued into 2009. With dollars behind them, Canada's athletes are proving to the world that Canadians can win on the international stage.

Meanwhile, our summer athletes are singing a different tune. Funding for the Road to Excellence program is significantly lower than what was originally requested. The next international multi-sport summer sporting event in Canada is a distant unknown. Let's not forget that the COC sold its marketing rights to VANOC to help finance the high cost of staging the Vancouver 2010 Games. Furthermore, in an environment in which Canada's focus is on the 2010 Olympics, few sponsors are seeing value in promoting the nation's Summer Olympians.

"Winter sport is getting substantially more money for us to be the best nation in Vancouver, which is understandable," said Les Gramantik, then the head coach of Athletics Canada, in an interview with the *Toronto Star*. "However, (there's) a total discrepancy between what winter sports and summer sports are getting."

Consider the plight of boxing, arguably one of Canada's most prolific summer sports, having yielded a total of six Olympic medals from 1988 to

1996 and having produced sporting legends like Willie Dewitt, Shawn O'Sullivan, and Lennox Lewis. In 1995, the government of Canada financed sport to the tune of $47 million per annum, of which $468,000 went to the sport of boxing. By 2006, sport funding had nearly tripled to $140 million per annum, but only $413,000 of that went to the Canadian Boxing Association, a decrease of nearly 11 percent. As for corporate sponsorship, that has been reduced to almost nil.

Canada's badminton players saw program funding cuts of over $20,000 in the six-year period ending in 2007, despite a 50-percent increase in federal sport funding during this same time span. Adding salt to Badminton Canada's wounds is the fact that the sport has no corporate sponsors to ease the financial burden resulting from the funding cuts.

Or how about our wrestlers? The men's budget was approximately $260,000 in 2007, according to the sport's president, Clive Llewellyn, whose organization took a $120,000 budget cut in February 2008 because Sport Canada didn't see medal potential in the sport. "You take out $120,000 — that has almost halved it," he says.

When funding to Canada's summer sport organizations is slashed, the onus falls on Canada's athletes to fund the shortfall. In today's sporting environment, our summer athletes are being asked not only to pay their own way to attend world championship events, but also to finance the cost of preparing for the Olympic Games. Ari Taub, a Greco-Roman wrestler at the 2008 Olympic Games, spent nearly $140,000 of his own money to prepare for the Games, because the Canadian Amateur Wrestling Association didn't have the funds to support all of its athletes. Bob Milroy, a badminton player, spent nearly $200,000 of his own money to prepare for Athens, only to suffer at the hands of the COC and their restrictive top-twelve standard. Milroy ended up watching the Games at home.

A kitchen-table system

VANOC CEO Furlong says that under Canada's present sporting system, some sports are highly organized while others are "managed off of the kitchen table," adding, "We have to improve that."

With an unlimited supply of funds at their disposal, winter sport officials have been busy trying to professionalize Canada's winter sport organizations. While there have been momentary lapses, the news surrounding Canada's winter athletes has primarily been on their unprecedented success on the field of play.

In contrast, faced with a dwindling supply of resources, our summer sport organizations are poorly organized; the individuals managing them appear unqualified; the coaches are accountable to no one; and the country's summer athletes are bearing the burden.

Consider the case of Karine Sergerie. Although she won a silver medal at the 2003 World Taekwondo Championships and was the reigning national champion in Canada, she ended up suing her sport organization after being told that she could not compete at the 2004 Summer Olympics. Patrice M. Brunet, the judge who presided over the case, stated, "By admission from all parties ... Karine Sergerie is the best athlete in her category; however, she will not attend the next Summer Olympic Games because she did not participate in a regional event ... This does not make sense ... (however) it is not for this panel to rewrite the rules ..."

Sergerie was not alone. In the twelve months leading up the 2004 Olympics, there were more than twelve cases in which athletes sought legal action as the result of a decision made by their respective summer sport organization. And it didn't stop four years later. In 2008, Megan Poss sued Syncro Canada over its selection process in determining the 2008 Olympic team. At issue was how coaches and officials were allowed to change the rules at any time. Poss eventually lost her appeal, but Michel G. Picher, the arbitrator who presided over the case, noted that athletes were being drawn into a process in which appeals and litigation were unavoidable.

In stark contrast, the number of lawsuits filed on behalf of Canada's winter athletes in the twelve-month lead-up to the 2006 Winter Olympics was nil, nada, nothing. With an influx of money from corporate sponsors and government agencies alike, Canada's winter sport system has professionalized itself. The organizations, for the most part, are managed by people who understand sport. Internationally acclaimed coaches have been hired to teach the athletes, and consultants have been hired to handle external concerns. It hasn't hurt either to have an organization like WinSport Canada hovering in the background to ensure that everything is managed accordingly.

"We are definitely set up better than we have ever been," Olympic speed skater Clara Hughes said. "I think each one of us has what we need and has the support we need."

Meanwhile, marathoner Nicole Stevenson, in an article in the *Saskatoon StarPhoenix*, summed up the sentiment of Canada's summer athletes with these words: "If Canada isn't proud of me, why should I beg to wear the Canadian uniform?"

13

Stop the Whining: Sharing the Blame, Heading for Fame

Working hand-in-hand with Tracy and Melanie, Al Morrow put together a winter training program composed of three weeks of intense dry-land training followed by seven days of on-the-water training in Florida. Tracy and Melanie were well aware that the cost of the Florida training sessions would come out of their own pockets, but the Olympics were coming and they knew that no price tag could be put on Olympic Gold.

With the thawing of ice in London, Ontario, in April, training moved from land to water. Three workouts a day, six days a week, became the norm. With only seventeen weeks until the start of the Olympics, Tracy and Melanie rowed over two hundred kilometres per week, spending upward of five hours per day together in a boat the width of a shoebox. Rain, wind, or sun, the twosome were out on the shores of Fanshawe Lake each morning at 7:30, preparing their boats for their first ninety-minute session of the day.

Then, at 11 a.m., after a short break at a breakfast diner, Tracy and Melanie were back on the water for their second row of the day. Lunch and some needed rest would follow, but the day was not over. A third row was the afternoon norm.

The two rowers knew they had to be prepared for everything and be able to respond when called on. This was the hope, and until the start of the Olympics, this was their focus.

The sport of rowing is about precision. Over a 2000-metre race that consists of 240 to 260 strokes, the smallest imperfection can make the difference between winning and losing. Tracy and Melanie understood this and in the lead-up to the Olympic Games, every detail of the race was broken down.

The all-important start — the first ten strokes of the race — set everything in order for the 2000 metres of hell that followed. The next fifty strokes are an all-out sprint, and as odd as it may sound, rowers then have to find a way to complete the remaining 1500 metres. Through the 500-metre mark, the idea is to relax and conserve energy for the final flurry, but at over forty strokes per minute, this is more difficult than it sounds.

Tracy and Melanie knew they had to be in contention with the leaders to the halfway mark, otherwise the race was over. For those in contention, the 1000-metre mark simply represents the start of the real race. Strategy and experience take over from there. Some crews start their push for the finish with 800 metres remaining; others wait. Regardless of strategy, with the race for first on the line, it wasn't uncommon to see stroke rates above forty-five per minute.

By the time the final beep sounded to mark the end of the race, Tracy and Melanie would have taxed their bodies to a level of pain that few Canadians could ever comprehend.

~

If whining were an official Olympic sport, Canada's Summer Olympians would be Olympic champions. Nobody does it better.

We need more cash, we're not treated fairly, it's too hot, it's too cold, there are too many hangers-on, there aren't enough hangers-on, we're sick, we're tired.

So are Canadians. We don't want to hear it anymore. We're tired of hearing that our summer athletes don't have enough funding to compete. In Athens, after Lori-Ann Muenzer won Olympic Gold in cycling, all we heard was how she lived on $16,000 a year while borrowing wheels from other nations at the 2004 Olympics. And how her coach, Steen Madsen, was reduced to coaching Muenzer from home in Canada via cell phone between races.

A similar sob story was heard from Olympic silver medallist Tonya Verbeek when she returned from Athens. "The day I got back from the Olympics, I went to stay at my parents' house. The phone started ringing with calls, mostly from the news media, first thing in the morning and it didn't stop all day," Verbeek told the *Toronto Sun*. "I went from that, to working a bingo to raise funds for my wrestling club."

After the Games in Athens, the crying continued. "I've been working for my country for eleven years as an athlete, and I'm not getting anything for it," said thirty-two-year-old fencer Sherraine Schalm.

"I think these athletes have to be elevated above the level of being charity cases," said Chris Rudge, CEO of the Canadian Olympic Committee, in an interview with the *Vancouver Sun*. "They have the right to be seen as people who are significant contributors to the welfare of this country."

In 2005, Statistics Canada classified anyone earning less than $20,778 per year as living below the poverty line. In 2006, nearly all of the over fourteen hundred Canadian athletes receiving a monthly tax-free stipend from the federal government earned less than $20,778. Elite, international-level competitors qualify for government funding. They earn $1,500 a month. Those deemed to be *potential* podium-bound international athletes earn $900 a month.

But don't tell Canadian taxpayers that they aren't doing their part. In 2007 alone, $165 million was invested by the federal government in amateur sport initiatives. Over $15 million of that went to fund the Own the Podium program, another $120 million to fund Canada's national and multi-sport programs, and another $20 million went to our amateur athletes themselves.

And don't forget that Vancouver is hosting the 2010 Olympics and all three levels of government are contributing significantly to the hosting of these Games. In preparation for these Games, British Columbia taxpayers alone are being asked to pay upward of $2.5 billion, according to a report by the province's auditor general.

Despite what our sport leaders would like us to believe, Canadian taxpayers are not at fault for the lack of funding for summer sport initiatives. The problem, rather, is that those managing sport in our country have chosen to invest monies on things like administration, the construction of winter sport facilities, and most importantly the goal of making this country the number-one *winter* sporting nation in the world.

And while we are on the issue of funding, Canadians are tired of seeing their summer athletes and organizations come to them practically begging for money when it is evident that they don't have their affairs in order. They are tired of seeing their summer athletes fight these battles on the front pages of the country's newspapers.

Canadians want to see winners and that's what they're seeing in the country's winter sport programs. This is why the country's winter athletes are national celebrities, shown on billboards and televisions across the country as preparations are being made for the 2010 Games in Vancouver and Whistler. Meanwhile, our summer athletes are as recognizable as Waldo on a street-side mural.

Canada's summer athletes do have a number of things to complain about. Unfortunately, they have been a little too forthcoming in sharing their sporting ills. Over the course of the past few years, Canadians have read the editorials in newspapers across the country, they've heard the cries for help, and at some point during all of this they have probably even sympathized with our poor deprived athletes. But enough already, is their attitude. Stop crying and do something about it.

14

Going Against the Current: Change Must Come from Within

After months of preparation, Tracy and Melanie were ready to put their training to the test. By June 2008, they were heading overseas for a four-week European tour. The trip would give them a firsthand take on where they ranked against the world's top lightweight women.

First up were the famed waters of the Rotsee in Lucerne, Switzerland, for the second leg of the World Cup Circuit. (The two had decided to skip the first world cup race of the year.) A third-place finish confirmed that the training program was working.

After Lucerne, the two and their coach, Al Morrow, headed north to train and race in the Netherlands, at the Bosbaan, the national training centre of the Dutch team. As the 2008 European Football Championship consumed the attention of much of the continent, Tracy and Melanie managed to stay focused. Two solid weeks of training alongside the Danish National Rowing Team and a first-place finish at a local regatta reassured the two that their Olympic preparations were progressing nicely.

Next up was the third and final leg of the 2008 world cup rowing season, in Poznan, Poland. This was a smaller affair than the Lucerne World Cup a few weeks earlier, with many of the world's top crews opting out of the event. Tracy and Melanie proved to be the class of the field, winning gold.

On the way home, the two and their coach reflected on a successful trip. The results from the European tour confirmed that they were in the hunt. With the Olympic Games now only a matter of weeks away, Tracy and Melanie were eager to get back to work and shave off those extra seconds that might make all the difference.

~

U.S. president John F. Kennedy famously said, "Ask not what your country can do for you, but what you can do for your country." Some forty years after he said this, Canada's amateur athletes have seemingly forgotten the meaning of that now legendary message. As the Beijing Olympics approached, Canada's summer athletes were once again asking Canadians to support them in their quest for Olympic glory. "Summer sport has waited long enough for additional funding and can't wait any longer," said Iain Brambell, chair of the coc's Athletes' Council and a three-time Olympian in the sport of rowing. "With the Olympic Games in Beijing less than eighteen months away, summer athletes need additional training and competition support — now."

Since that time, Canadians have come forward and given the Road to Excellence plan $72 million to support summer athletes in their quest for glory. This, however, is less than 15 percent of the requested $510 million needed to give our athletes the services they require. To help fund the shortfall and make that step forward toward Olympic glory, Canada's summer athletes need to stop looking to others for remedies and start asking what they can do themselves to improve their situation.

However, the experience of Canada's athletes over the past two decades suggests that this may be a lot harder than it sounds.

The Athletes<small>CAN</small> experiment

Athletes<small>CAN</small>, an independent organization designed to service the needs of Canada's amateur athletes, was introduced in 1992, based on the desire of Canada's amateur athletes to have their own voice separate from Canada's sporting brass. The organization was formed under the leadership of Ann Peel, a race walker on Canada's track and field team. It consisted of a small independent group of athletes, including Olympic gold medallist Kay Worthington in rowing, Olympic medallist Steve Podborski in alpine skiing, and Dan Thompson in aquatics. At the time, the voice of Canada's amateur athletes was the Athletes' Council, which was part of the Canadian Olympic Committee.

As Peel puts it, after the Ben Johnson steroid scandal of 1988, the athletes wanted to write a report to the Dubin Commission, the lengthy investigation that ensued in Canada. "We presented it to the Canadian Olympic Committee for their review, who proceeded to slip it under the carpet."

Following the Dubin Commission, Peel and her group recognized that they were all affected by the same issues. "Dan Thompson, the captain, was kicked off the swim team for standing up for one of his teammates," she says. "Steve Podborski was told he couldn't cycle in the off-season, and we all lacked the funding we required. We started realizing how divergent the athletes' voice was from the Canadian Olympic Committee."

In 1993, a year after the formation of Athletes<small>CAN</small>, Canada's amateur athletes held their first Athletes Forum, gathering athletes from all corners of the country to network, share ideas, learn about the sport system, and develop leadership skills.

As the first such organization of its kind, Athletes<small>CAN</small> hit the Canadian sports landscape with a bang, demanding increased funding for Canada's athletes and better representation within the country's sporting organizations. "In those first few years we were radical, not nice, and did a lot of things right," says Peel. "In 1995, athletes received their first carding increase in over ten years and Sport Solution was created to provide athletes with legal information and assistance. We filed appeals on behalf of athletes and demonstrated to sport organizations that athletes had rights."

Many of the programs created by Peel and her group continue to exist today, some seventeen years later. Sport Solution, a not-for-profit program, helps Canada's amateur athletes resolve legal conflicts. And the Athletes Forum, gathering Canada's amateur athletes for a weekend-long conference, remains the organization's flagship event.

Today, AthletesCAN is only a shadow of its former self. Following Peel's departure in 1996, the organization shifted its focus and began to build a bridge between itself and the Canadian sport system. "They were less outspoken, part of a system, and not as strong an advocate for Canada's athletes," says Peel. "I don't think they are serving Canada's athletes well."

Sleeping with the enemy

In fact, many within AthletesCAN are working for those they are supposed to protect the athletes from. In October 2006, Claire Carver-Dias, a medallist at the Sydney Olympics in the sport of synchronized swimming, was elected president of AthletesCAN while also serving as program manager of the COC's Athlete and Community Relations Committee. She has since left the COC but went on to work as a director of communications with Bobsleigh Canada Skeleton. Lori Johnstone, former president of AthletesCAN, recognizes that while Claire is trusted and well liked by her peers, she faces real and perceived conflicts in her job.

Peel agrees, noting that "it isn't possible to retain independence when you are staff to a sport of any kind, no matter how liked and respected you are. Can you imagine an Exxon employee being the volunteer president of the World Wildlife Fund or a climate change organization? Obviously not. To have an effective, independent voice, you cannot compromise your independence by connecting advocacy with your need for a career. The career has to come first. That is why it is always so important that athletic leadership retain its independence from the sporting system."

Unfortunately, this has not happened. Iain Brambell was a director with AthletesCAN and an executive director with BC Athlete Voice, an organization designed to give high-performing athletes a collective voice. At the same time, he served as an executive board member with the Canadian Olympic Committee: the same organization that nearly destroyed the efforts of one of amateur athletes' most adoring supporters, Jane Roos and her See You In ... fund.

In her first ten years, Roos and her fund helped support over five hundred amateur athletes in their preparation for Summer and Winter Olympiads. Brambell was among those who received funding from the fund after sending an e-mail stating that he "was an unemployed rower ... and needed her (Roos') support more than ever." When approached for his thoughts on the potential conflict of interest between protecting the interests of Canada's amateur athletes and those of the Canadian Olympic Committee, Brambell said he couldn't discuss the matter because of his affiliation with the COC.

Michael Smith was the president of AthletesCAN while attending the 2004 Olympic Games in Athens as part of the COC's mission staff. Those were the same Games that had forty-seven eligible Canadian athletes watching the Olympics unfold from their living rooms back home because the COC decided to make Canada's qualifying standards for the Athens Games more difficult than the international standard.

Karen Purdy was a board member of both AthletesCAN and the COC at the time of those Games. She defended the COC's restrictive top-twelve qualifying standard, claiming in an interview that mediocre Canadian athletes were using the Olympics as a vacation. She also noted that these athletes simply partied and used up medical services that better athletes needed more urgently. AthletesCAN's official position on the matter was that the decision lacked merit and tarnished the spirit and values of the Olympic ideal.

Peel, now a high-ranking lawyer, is angry at the organization she helped create. "Today, if someone wants a career in sports administration, they use AthletesCAN as a stepping-stone, compromising their ability to be an effective critic ... I end up advising about twenty-five athletes per year who come to me for assistance. It distresses me when I hear their stories and frustration with the organization that was created to deal with these issues ... I feel sad that the organization we worked so hard to create has moved from advocate to co-option and effective merger with the COC."

Hiding from the hard questions

The Olympic qualifying event for the mistral class in sailing was the 2004 Mistral World Championships, held in Turkey April 8-18, 2004. Athletes sent the COC a letter the previous February requesting a different qualifying event because of political instability in the Middle East at the time and the difficulty of obtaining sufficient coaching support. The COC responded that they would change the qualifying event only if the Canadian government posted a travel advisory for that area.

A month later, Dominique Vallee sent the COC a second request to change the qualifying event, this time because a foot injury sustained during training had rendered her incapable of competing at the championships. At the time of her request, alternative events were available and acceptable for selection purposes. However, the COC didn't respond in time and the events passed. As a result of the COC's delay, Vallee asked for an exemption from the requirements for selection to Canada's Olympic Team. The COC declined her request, even though she was regarded as Canada's best athlete in the sport and exempting her would penalize no other athlete.

Frustrated throughout the process, Vallee called Thomas Jones, the executive director of AthletesCAN at the time. Vallee says that after a lengthy conversation, she was told to write Jones a letter. He would look into the matter and get back to her. Vallee wrote the letter but says her concerns were never addressed. Credited for strengthening alliances with the Canadian Olympic Committee during his three-year tenure with AthletesCAN, Jones was promoted to CEO of Commonwealth Games Canada, in January 2005. Meanwhile, Vallee, a prominent athlete with an unlimited future in the sport, seriously considered retiring from sport altogether. "I was burned by my federation, burned by the COC," she says.

Fortunately for Canada, she continued to pursue her goals, winning gold at the 2007 Pan American Games. However, unlike 2004, this time around Vallee was not naïve enough to think politics would not get in her way again. "After 2004 I thought about what I could do to change (things)," she notes. "I recognized that AthletesCAN can do a lot." She adds that with a board structure in place, along with money, AthletescAN has the ability to impact sport federations and the coc. Following through on her wish to make amateur sport "more fair" to all athletes, she accepted the nomination of her peers to the organization's board in late 2004.

However, athletes like Vallee who strive to make a difference are an exception. Randy Starkman of the *Toronto Star* notes that many recently retired athletes are so fed up after their career is over that they want nothing to do with sport, while most of this country's current crop of athletes are satisfied with the little they get. "Perhaps that's part of the problem," he says.

"We're caught up in political correctness and all this s—," said former Olympic swim coach Dean Boles in an interview with the *Toronto Star*. "I think it hurts us."

Lori Johnstone, past president of AthletescAN, acknowledges that leaders within the organization have talked about recruiting strong members. She adds that there have to be people who are "willing and prepared to ask the hard questions and contribute to building solutions." Guy Tanguay, cEO of AthletescAN, agrees, saying, "There is a whole group of alumni that has to get involved."

The problem is — they aren't doing so. Many of Canada's amateur athletes are afraid to speak out for fear of ostracizing themselves within their sport. Meanwhile, Canada's sporting alumni look at the hardships that Canada's amateur athletes endure as a rite of passage.

Jane Roos, founder of the See You In ... fund, says that getting amateur sport alumni to speak out on the state of amateur sport in Canada is next to impossible. "There is an attitude among Canada's alumni of 'if I had to endure it, you will, too.'"

All of which has left a leadership void among Canada's amateur athletes.

A slippery slope of complacency

Canada's summer athletes face a number of major issues in the upcoming years. With the Vancouver 2010 Games coming, there is a skewing of priorities for summer and winter sport in Canada. There is a lack of sport infrastructure.

The management of Canada's summer sport organizations has been called into question. Then there are the concerns about balancing participation and high-performance priorities and so on.

Canada's summer athletes assume that someone will take care of these issues for them. While this may be true, the wrong people are doing so. Rachel Corbett of the Centre of Sport and Law acknowledges that the representatives who represent the interests of Canada's amateur athletes are completely ineffective. "Often they don't have the time, don't have the knowledge, and don't have the commitment to properly represent the concerns of Canada's athletes." Corbett adds that "the business of sport governance is pretty dull and it is often the last thing athletes want to do."

Lori Johnstone, a past president of AthletesCAN, adds that a slippery slope of complacency exists among Canada's amateur athletes.

In any case, Canada's sport organizations are using the athletes' indifference to their advantage. Every day across Canada, athletes willingly forfeit their rights in perpetuity by agreeing to the terms and conditions of an athlete agreement — a legal contract between the athletes and their own sport organization. Sport organizations, in turn, are using these rights to their advantage by forging marketing relationships with sponsors.

Guy Tanguay, CEO of AthletesCAN, acknowledges that problems exist with the athletes' agreement. He notes that, to mitigate these issues, his organization provides items that athletes should be aware of before signing on the dotted line. However, the Centre for Sport and Law in Canada states that these standard-form agreements have evolved into full-fledged commercial contracts, exceeding, in some cases, seventy-five pages in length. The Centre says that few athletes have the knowledge or the financial capacity to negotiate a commercial contract and then are told by their federations that they need to sign on the dotted line.

Rachel Corbett at the Centre for Sport and Law, the person responsible for drafting many of these agreements on behalf of Canada's sporting organizations, notes that "athletes are at a totally uneven bargaining power when it comes to these agreements. National sport organizations have the athlete over a barrel."

Maybe so, but imagine if every athlete agreed to throw the athlete agreement aside. Athletes would suddenly have a bargaining position to negotiate from.

Such a move is unlikely, however. Peel herself acknowledges that Canada's amateur athletes don't seem to care about the issues. "The fight is gone from the athletes."

Dominique Vallee, a windsurfer and former director with AthletesCAN, says, "For much of their lives, athletes are told when to eat, when to sleep, how to train, when to train, and so on. As a result, it's tough to get leadership at the athlete level ... Athletes run by the rules, believe in authority, and are afraid to speak out."

And because athletes are afraid to speak out, they give up their rights to market themselves during national championships, world championships, Commonwealth Games, and the Olympic Games. An athlete gets little in return, but year in, year out, like sheep led to the slaughter, they sign their documents, many doing so without first reading them, forgetting that these are legally binding contracts.

However, what Canada's amateur athletes are failing to realize is that their indifference toward athletic matters is hurting them. Peel says that athletic resources are even scarcer today than in the 1990s. This despite the fact that funding for Canadian Amateur Sport has more than doubled since 1999. "It pisses me off," she says.

In a study conducted by AthletesCAN back in 2004, 50 to 60 percent of Canadian athletes said that money posed a medium to large barrier for them. Furthermore, the overriding concern drawn from the study was the level of financial assistance that athletes receive.

Why? Not because of a lack of funding from government or taxpayers themselves, but because Canada's amateur athletes are willing to forgo their rights. Meanwhile, sport organizations, as we will see, aren't capitalizing on their acquired marketing rights to promote athletes in Canada. Sponsors, as a result, are conspicuously absent in Summer Olympic sport. And it is the athlete who suffers the consequences.

15

The Olympic Games: Tracy's View

Author's note: This chapter is based on e-mails from Tracy Cameron detailing the challenges of competition at the 2008 Beijing Olympic Games.

～

After years of anticipation, we are just days away from the beginning of the biggest athletic event of my life. Everyone has been asking, "Are you excited?" and "What's it like?"

First let me take you back a few weeks. Al Morrow, our coach, has been to seven Olympic Games and has had numerous successful crews along the way, so I have total faith in our program and his ability to lead us to peak performance. I mentioned in my last e-mail that we were reaching a point where all the hard work was done and we were entering the fine-tuning phase. Okay, I may have been wrong about the hard work thing. Little did I know then that we were about to enter another loading (a.k.a. killer) phase. Nevertheless, I am happy to report that we survived. The 1x2000m (rowing races are 2000m in length) will be easy after what we've just been through in practices.

Aside from the workouts, I have to say that Al was brilliant in his approach to our mental preparation and getting us ready for what we are about to experience here in Beijing. A few times a week the three of us (Mel, Al, and I) would sit down for breakfast and have a roundtable discussion. It was during these breakfast talks that the excitement began to mount for me. Topics included beliefs (about ourselves and our competitors), incentives, and how to maintain the positive energy and keep it *fun* (one of my favourites). It never failed: After every meeting, my step was a little lighter, and I became more and more excited about heading to the start line.

Fast forward: We've made it! We have settled into our hotel; we aren't staying in the village, because our venue is an hour's drive from of the city. Because we arrived early, we've been able to create an environment at the venue where it feels like our home turf. So we already feel very comfortable in our surroundings and it's back to business as usual. We are removed from the main hub in the city, but we made the trek into the village on Sunday, so we were able to experience a bit of the magic that makes the Olympics different from any other regatta. But that is a story for tomorrow.

A glimpse of village life

As I mentioned yesterday, although we are not living in the village because it is too far from our venue, on Sunday we were fortunate enough to explore the facilities. The enormousness of it was overwhelming: an area of sixty-six hectares that's home to sixteen thousand athletes and officials.

The main hub, or international zone, boasts a plethora of facilities and services. If you need a haircut or your nails done, no worries, just pop into the salon. Need a bank, a florist, dry cleaner, merchandise, post office/courier centre, mobile phone, photo shop, Internet café, movie theatre, or perhaps even a ticket office to book future travel? Again, no problem. It's all right there and ours for the taking.

If you are a video analysis junkie, then you can get more than your fix at the sport-tech centre in the Canadian house. They have a room that is dedicated to all incoming video footage from every venue at all times. The video streams are then filed and categorized, accessible for review. So let's say I'm on the soccer team and I'm playing Portugal tomorrow and I want to know more about #19, a striker. I could sit down at my handy computer, punch in #19, and every video clip with her in it would be at my fingertips. I dare not attempt to describe the other analytical and technological capabilities that can be accessed from this room, because my lack of understanding in this area would not do them justice.

The final honourable mention is the dining hall. *Oh my goodness.* Can I just say heaven on earth? I'm not kidding! It's the size of a football field. Upon entry, you have to pause to decide which way to go. If you choose to go right you enter the Mediterranean Cuisine section with all the freshest fruits and veggies you can imagine, along with nicely grilled meats. If you choose to go left you end up in the Asian Cuisine section, with your choice of local fare. Or if you simply walk straight ahead, you enter the International Cuisine Section, where you find the staples of any diet.

In addition to the different ethnic cuisine zones, the dessert section is centrally located and does not discriminate between nationalities ... let's face it, dessert is universal! Finally, if you have a craving for a Big Mac, McDonald's has staked a claim at the far end of the building. Melanie has already claimed that she will be frequenting the joint to indulge in McFlurries during the second week (when all is said and done). Perhaps I will join her. (A girl's gotta dream!)

The heats

Well, I'm getting ready for bed; it's the night before. Crazy. We are ready, confident, and poised. Quickly, here are the details of the race:

Lane One   — Great Britain (fast off the start, typically fall off pace after the 1000)
Lane Two   — Greece (slow off start but increase in speed down the course)
Lane Three   — Canada ...

Lane Four	— Germany (fast starters, consistent through the body, always hangin' around)
Lane Five	— South Africa (not strong contenders)
Lane Six	— Finland (steady, even, solid crew, not sprinters)
Race time	— 3 p.m. in Beijing (3 a.m. in Ontario)

Weather prediction — headwind, chance of rain, slightly cooler temperature = slower race times.

That's all for now! Thank you all for your best wishes and support; you can count on me bringing that energy into the boat tomorrow.

The heat recap

Our thanks to all you crazy people who set alarms to get up in the wee hours of the morning at home to cheer us on. Also, thank you to all who cheered us on while enjoying the replays over a nice cup of java.

We are pleased to have come in the top two, finishing second to Germany in our heat. This puts us directly into the semi on Thursday. It is always nice to avoid one race, the repachage (a second chance of sorts for those countries who finished third or lower in their heat). Just having the first race under our belts is excellent. We may have been a little excited, but now we've got the jitters out and are well under way in preparing for the next phase.

We've done our video review/analysis, we've rehashed the race, we've determined a few key things to focus on, and now we are looking forward to our next opportunity on Thursday. We will know the draw after the reps tomorrow.

The semi's

Semifinal LW2x at 3:40 p.m Thursday; top three will advance to the final.

Lane 1 — Japan
Lane 2 — USA

Lane 3 — Australia
Lane 4 — China
Lane 5 — Canada
Lane 6 — Greece

What can I say? We are getting to the point where good crews will not make it through. I expect it to be a barn burner. No one in this race will concede; they are all tough competitors and will never, never, never let off until after they've crossed the line. So, having said all of that, Mel and I are focused and are taking a task-oriented approach to the race. After the heats we identified a few key technical points that we will emphasize tomorrow. We will be relentless, we will stay focused, we will execute our plan, and we will allow the boat to do the job it was designed to do (run with speed and efficiency).

Okay, time for bed!

The Big Kahuna

Well, my friends, we finished first in our semifinal and have advanced to the final. Today is the day! It's the day that I have been dreaming of since I was a little girl. Who knew that on the day of my Olympic final I'd be sipping my coffee solo at 4:30 a.m., watching the sun come up in Beijing in total peace and harmony?

Over the past seventy-two hours I have experienced major emotions that are hard to describe. I've gone from having feelings of wanting to run away, simply saying to Al and Mel, "Well it's been a slice; thanks for the good times, I'm outta here," to "All right, I feel unstoppable, let's get 'er goin.'" Yesterday when I heard that many crews/athletes had to pull out of racing due to a stomach bug, I basically turned into a hypochondriac and started taking on physiological symptoms. When I started to logically analyse the situation, I realized that my discomfort may have been caused by the copious amounts of coffee that I had consumed that day. After a hot bath and some neutral food, homoeostasis returned to the underworld.

So, am I ready? I looked back in my journal and realized that I hadn't missed a single practice this year; I have not had to deal with injury; I have a strong partner; we have done the training that has produced champions; we have a coach who is at his eighth Olympic Games and has prepared us for every possible scenario; we have a phenomenal support team; I have a company (Midnight Oil & Daylight Energy) who have backed me financially since the beginning of this journey, who have taken care of my day-to-day worries of "Where is the money going to come from for this month's rent and groceries?"; I have piles and piles of people who believe in me and have faith that I have what it takes to bring home the gold; we have faced every single crew in this final and we know their tactics and have confidence in our own; I know how to sing *O Canada* in both French and English.

Am I ready? Hell, yeah!

Thank you all sooooooo much for sharing my journey.

16

All for One and One for All: Putting the Fight Back into Our Athletes

Every year from September to February, American football dominates the television. One has to wonder if Canada's summer sport organizations couldn't do the same. After all, a little less than forty years ago, football was virtually unknown to the American public.

A question of marketing

In 1960, when Pete Rozelle was appointed commissioner of the NFL, there were only twelve teams in the league, each worth about $1 million. When he left, in 1989, there were twenty-eight teams, each one worth more than $100 million, making the NFL the undisputed king of American sport. According to Bill Reynolds of the *Providence Journal*, Rozelle transformed football by understanding the power of television. He understood marketing. Most of all, he understood that football wasn't a sport; it was a business.

One of Rozelle's first initiatives was moving the NFL's head office from suburban Philadelphia to downtown New York, where the money was. A year later, he negotiated a league-wide television agreement with CBS for $9.2 million that replaced individual television packages for each of the twelve teams. The league hasn't looked back, and today U.S. networks pay over $3 billion per annum to televise the sport.

Meanwhile, in Canadian sport, there isn't an amateur sport organization to be found in Canada's most populous city, Toronto. Canada's headquarters for Summer Olympic sport is located in Ottawa, a government town. Compare this with Winter Olympic sport, which has its Canadian headquarters in Calgary, arguably Canada's wealthiest city.

Through the power of the Internet, the public can watch clips of American football teams' press conferences, past games, and even practices. Sport fans are tied in almost 24/7 to the ongoing happenings of their favourite teams. The NFL has recognized that we are living in the midst of a communications revolution with an unprecedented opportunity to promote and market sport in new and exciting ways.

If only the same were true here in Canada. Surf the web pages of Canada's summer sport organizations. Video streaming — catering to a huge cross-section of sport fans — is non-existent. Audio clips are still a novelty. Blogs by coaches and athletes about their daily trials are conspicuously absent. Athlete profiles are dated. Information is a virtual luxury to amateur sport fans, and even the local media have a hard time determining dates for upcoming events.

Winter sport organizations don't fare much better. Only international hockey and, to a lesser extent, figure skating events are rebroadcast through broad-band Internet on third-party websites hours later. Audio clips are tough to find, and the sites themselves are bland.

However, Canada's winter sport organizations are benefiting from the added publicity that comes with an Olympic Games on native soil. Government officials recognize it. That's why they are devoting the bulk of their financial resources to this initiative. Sponsors recognize it. They are paying billions of dollars to get their products affiliated with the Games.

A global business

Walt Macnee, executive director of the Canadian Athletes Now fund and president of global markets for MasterCard, notes that people perceive the Olympic Games as the "last great not-for-profit entertainment." But he notes that "the Olympics bring in money, they spend it, and there is a margin of profit. We as Canadians are duped into saying it is not a business, but it is and no one sees it." The Olympics are able to derive huge profits, largely because its global workforce is non-unionized, he says. "Like the National Hockey League owners of the 1960s who were able to bust the union movements of its workers, the Olympic movement realizes that if they keep its workers down they can get ridiculous fortunes off their backs. The Olympics are exploiting (our athletes') passion and love of sport and the result is that the athletes are getting their wages taken away from them." And nowhere is this more evident than in Canada.

As previously indicated, Canada's athletes forgo virtually all of their rights from the sporting bodies that represent them, including the right to market themselves. Sport organizations, in turn, use the athletes' visibility to form marketing relationships with their sponsors. The COC is doing something similar. Athletes are accepting of the situation because they know sponsorship money helps provide the resources they require to succeed.

Government officials and the sporting organizations that are supporting them are investing a substantial amount of money into the efforts of Canada's winter athletes. Meanwhile, all Canada's summer athletes can do is eat the scraps their winter cousins leave behind.

To add salt to the wounds of the country's summer athletes, VANOC owns the marketing rights to the Olympic Games here in Canada until 2012. As a result, high-profile Olympic partnerships with the likes of Rona, Air Canada, and Royal Bank are almost exclusively devoted to our winter athletes.

And if that wasn't enough, Canada's summer sport organizations are marketing our athletes as though it was the 1950s. TV coverage of sporting events is almost nil, video-streaming is virtually unknown, and the Internet isn't being used to its potential.

"In Canada, athletes pretend that sport is a pure uncorrupted game, but there is a business element to it," says Macnee. A business element whereby companies like Hudson's Bay, Petro-Canada, Birks, Air Canada, and General Motors have donated nearly a billion dollars to be a part of the Olympic movement in Canada. And Canada's athletes have to understand this.

Fight!

In a sport system where Canada's summer athletes are void of the necessary financial resources to succeed, lack the basic employment rights that Canadians have come to expect, have little or no legal rights, and have no bargaining power; in a sport system where dollars are devoted to getting our winter athletes onto the podium at the expense of our summer athletes; in a sport system where Canada's summer sport organizations lack the necessary resources, coaching, and facilities to get our summer athletes onto the podium, it may seem surprising to hear that Canada's summer athletes have the power to change everything.

For evidence supporting this, the country's athletes need look no further than the actions of fellow athletes before them. In an article written for the *Daily Miner News*, Bob Stewart wrote of a tiff between former curling champion Ed (The Wrench) Werenich and the Canadian curling establishment.

Stewart writes, "On the eve of the 1990 World Curling Championships, Werenich balked at the Canadian Curling Association's plan to designate one of their executives as his team coach and send him along with the team, at the association's expense, to the world championships in Sweden.

"No way, said the Wrench. He didn't like the guy selected, and furthermore, if there was cash for a fifth team member, he wanted to hold it in reserve for his spare in case of injury to one of his normal foursome. If the association wanted to give someone a free ride on the public dime, they were welcome to do so, but not as part of his squad."

In the end, the association caved to Werenich's ultimatum that he would pull out.

More recently, in the United States, six snowboarders led by 2002 Olympic gold medallist Ross Powers broke away from the U.S. snowboarding federation to form a group called The Collection. The purpose of this new group: to take advantage of endorsement opportunities outside their federation that didn't conflict with Olympic sponsorship agreements. They negotiated clothing and equipment deals with suppliers, made action films, and hawked everything from chocolate bars to snowboards. These elite boarders made upward of $500,000 per year, proof positive that Canada's summer athletes can make a difference.

Our athletes can get the resources they require if they work together and are willing to challenge the system. They can get their proportionate share of monies from the federal government. They can get sport organizations to manage their activities efficiently while getting the resources they require. They can lead the fight to get athletes on the podium. They can do all this and much more through a strong independent union. "Canada needs leadership from someone in the system to stand up and say 'union,'" says Macnee.

After all, unionization has proven to be effective for North America's professional athletes, especially those in Major League Baseball. Up to 1965, MLB players were bound to their respective clubs, which denied the players the same basic employment rights that people in other professions had long taken for granted. All this changed in 1965 with the hiring of Marvin Miller. Miller was a highly respected economist for the United Steelworkers of America. With his outside expertise, the fortunes of MLB players slowly began to change. Miller immediately began to mould players into a bona fide labour union. His first steps were to shore up the union's finances by beginning a group-licensing program and educating the players about the fundamentals of organizing and solidarity.

With a well-educated and organized membership, Miller changed the landscape of professional sports forever. During his tenure, from 1965 to 1983, base salaries, pension funds, licensing rights, and revenues were brought up to unprecedented levels. He helped negotiate the right to arbitration to resolve grievances while establishing free agency rights.

Since those early days, the average salary of a Major League Baseball player has gone from less than $100,000 in 1970 to nearly $3 million in 2005. In 2007 alone, $2.5 billion was allocated to player's salaries on annual revenues of over $6 billion.

Compare this with Canada's amateur sport system, where in 2007 slightly over $20 million was allocated to pay Canada's amateur athletes a monthly stipend. Meanwhile, according to Gordon Campbell, premier of British Columbia, the economic impact of the 2010 Vancouver Winter Games is expected to exceed $10 billion. The fact is, Canadian athletes are not getting their fair share because they are unorganized, ill-informed, and unaware of their rights.

The Major League Baseball Players Association (MLBPA) has negotiated a group-licensing program that utilizes the collective marketing power of players to assist licensees and sponsors wanting to associate their brands and products with the excitement that major leaguers can provide. Through an individual agreement with each player, the association holds the exclusive worldwide right to use, license, and sublicense the names, numbers, nicknames, likenesses, signatures, and other personal indicia (known as "publicity rights") of active MLB players.

Compare this with amateur sport, where the COC holds the worldwide right to license and sublicense the names, likenesses, signatures, nicknames, and publicity rights of Canada's Olympic athletes.

There is little question that when it comes to amateur sport, Canada's athletes have little or no rights. This needs to change, and the onus to do so lies directly on the athletes. Why would we expect the managers of Canada's amateur sport system to improve athletes' rights? Looking back at the history of our great nation, when the British North American Act prohibited women from being appointed to the Canadian Senate, it wasn't a man or government official who appealed the Supreme Court of Canada in 1929 to fight for women's equality. It was Canada's "famous five" — Henrietta Muir Edwards, Nellie McClung, Louise McKinney, Emily Murphy, and Irene Parlby — who helped guarantee that women were represented at all levels of Canadian politics. Similarly, someone within our current crop of athletes needs to lead the charge for the creation of an educated, united, and organized union for the country's amateur athletes.

Imagine the opportunities that could present themselves if Canada's amateur athletes came together as a collective voice and demanded change. Imagine an amateur sport system in which our athletes are given the financial resources they need, the resources they require, the coaching they want, and an approach that supports them every step of the way. Imagine a country that can succeed at both the 2010 Winter Games in Vancouver *and* the 2012 Olympic Summer Games in London.

Epilogue

The race was scheduled for 3:30 p.m. local time. With five minutes until the start of Tracy's race, Canadians were nervous for their Olympic idol. Even from half a world away, the pressure was unbearable.

The water in Beijing was calm, with not a ripple in sight. Aside from casual banter by television commentators, silence descended on the rowing venue. Forty-five thousand fans dressed in a dazzling array of colours held their breath as they waited for the race to start.

The combatants, meanwhile, appeared calm — as though they had each gone through this experience a million times before. The years of repetition had prepared each of the twelve athletes for this precise moment.

Finally, a voice echoed throughout the Shunyi Olympic Rowing and Canoeing Park. "Women's Lightweight Double Final," said the official starter from his perch high above the venue.

Each of the women sitting patiently in their respective lanes went through a final check-through of their boat. Gestures of encouragement were shared between the members of each pair. Tracy took a deep breath and then slowly readied herself for the race ahead. She appeared comfortable and seemed to be soaking up all the excitement around her.

Each of the six countries was slowly called to attention. The rowers gripped their oars a little tighter — and then ... the race began.

All six boats ripped out of the gates like gunshots, the women rowing up to forty-five strokes per minute, gasping for air. Tracy was battling for the lead. Some 500 metres into the race, she was in a dead heat, rowing at full capacity. Four boats were separated by a measly second.

Through the 1000-metre mark, she was fighting to break free from the pack, but the pack wouldn't let her leave. Each athlete was working at maximum capacity and the race for an Olympic medal was well under way.

With 500 metres to go, fatigue was starting to show on all the teams, but with the finish line now in sight, the final push was on. One could feel the roar of the crowd all the way back to Canada. The energy of the crowd was carrying each of the boats through the final few strokes.

At the end, four boats were fighting for three spots. Then the horn went. Each of the six teams screamed in agony. It was a photo finish.

The combatants waited. Time seemed to stand still until finally the results were displayed. Tracy and Melanie had finished third, beating Germany for the final spot on the podium by four one-hundreds of a second. Tracy was an Olympic medallist.

Tracy's feet haven't touched the ground since. Living the life of a rock star, she was seen at centre ice of the Toronto Maple Leafs home opener, has spoken to hundreds of admirers, and has partied like never before.

What the future holds is unknown. There are rumours that she wants to return to rowing, after some well-deserved time away from the sport, to pursue the one medal in four years' time that eludes her: Olympic Gold.

She has also made it clear that she wants to be the person who plants the seed of magic and belief into our future Olympians, so that they, too, can achieve their goals.

As we have seen, only a select few of our Summer Olympians can move forward in the belief that, like Tracy, they can win an Olympic medal. For the remainder, money, politics, coaching, facilities, and so on present obstacles that are simply too great. But don't think that these issues cannot be resolved. The success of Canada's Winter Olympic athletes on the international scene is proof positive that they can.

The task is no doubt a daunting one and likely controversial, but history reveals what happens when under-represented Canadians come together to create change. The labour movement of the 1880s, which gave workers around the world the right to fair wages, safe working conditions, and medical care; women's voting rights in the 1920s; and, most recently, the gay and lesbian movement, giving all Canadians, regardless of sexual orientation, the right to marry — these are examples of the power an under-represented segment of the Canadian public can have when they collectively fight for change.

And while it won't make international headlines and transform history, once Canada's amateur athletes come together, the opportunities will be endless.

With inspiring and successful athletes like Tracy Cameron planting the seed of hope into our future Olympians, now is the time for change.

Sources

Introduction
Publications

Success in Beijing has Canada aiming high in 2012, Vicki Hall, *Calgary Herald*, August 24, 2008.

1   A Nation Sinks Back in Disappointment — Again
Opening discussion
Websites

FISA, International Olympic Committee

Looking for a scapegoat
Discussions

Brian Richardson
Websites

Canadian Encyclopedia
Publications

Montgomery calls it off, Dave Fuller, *Toronto Sun*, September 27, 2000.

The winter-summer discrepancy
Discussions
Bob Storey
Websites, television
CBC Sports
Comments made by
Joseph S. Blatter: Canada sets U-20 World Cup attendance record, CBC Sports, July 20, 2007.
Publications
Bernard and Busse, Tuck School of Business at Dartmouth, July 2004.
Comments made by
Patricia Chafe: Canada is emerging as an Olympic powerhouse, Mark Sappenfield, *Christian Science Monitor*, February 23, 2006.
Chris Rudge: All that Glitters ..., Cam Cole, *National Post*, August 12, 2004.

Flagging athletes and preening politicians
Websites
Calgary Olympic Development Association, WinSport Canada
Publications
Turin will test program value: government funding an investment or a gamble? Paul Friesen, *Winnipeg Sun*, February 12, 2006.
Politicians get de luxe treatment at Olympics, James Christie, *Globe and Mail*, July 13, 2002.
Like other Countries Canada could pay the podium, Terry Jones, *Edmonton Sun*, February 19, 2006.
Comments made by
Canada's athletes: Ottawa to be lobbied for more Games cash, Jim Byers, *Toronto Star*, February 27, 2006.
Chris Rudge: Untitled, Alan Maki, *Globe and Mail*, July 5, 2003.
Diane Jones Konihowski: What's cookin' Diane?, Terry Jones, *Edmonton Sun*, September 10, 2000.
Michael Chambers: All that glitters ..., Cam Cole, *National Post*, August 12, 2004.

Our Olympic prospects
Websites
The Toque

Heading to Vancouver
Discussions
John Furlong
Websites
Globe and Mail
Comments made by
Alexander Ross: No longer afraid to be the best, Christie Blatchford, theglobeand mail.com, February 27, 2006.

Athletes must find their voice
Discussions
John Furlong
Websites
Canadian Olympic Committee
Publications
Right man to steer ship, Dave Stubbs, *National Post*, September 28, 2006.
Comments made by
Alex Baumann: Right man to steer ship, Dave Stubbs, *National Post*, September 28, 2006.

2 The New Ice Age: Things Weren't Always This Way

Opening discussion
Discussions
Tracy Cameron, Blair Rasmussen
Websites, television
cbc.ca Torino coverage
Leuders, Brown claim bobsled silver, Canadian Press, TSN website, February 19, 2006.
Publications
Crawford sprints to gold, Jim Byers, *Toronto Star*, February 22, 2006.
Scott and Renner give Canada a big boost at the Olympics with gutsy silver, Canadian Press, *Toronto Sun*, February 14, 2006.

Canada's Olympic History
Websites
Canadian Olympic Committee, Library and Archives Canada, McGill Athletics,

International Olympic Committee
Publications
Canada is emerging as an Olympic powerhouse, Mark Sappenfield, *Christian Science Monitor*, February 23, 2006.

The winter phoenix
Publications
Canada remains happily mediocre, Bruce Dowbiggin, *Calgary Herald*, August 26, 2008.

3   Rocky Mountain High: The Calgary Experience
Opening discussion
Discussions
Tracy Cameron, Bill France, John Mills, Gordon Ritchie
Websites
ctv.ca, WinSport Canada, CODA, Olympic Oval, cbc.ca
Olympic sport and education a unique mix at national sport school, Donna Spencer, cbc.ca

Chinook winds
Websites, television
cbc.ca, Cross Country Canada
Comments made by
Pierre Lueders: A new wave of Olympians has come of age, Tara Kimura, CBC Sports, February 11, 2006.
Beckie Scott: Beckie Scott retires from competitive cross country ski racing, Chris Dornan, *In Source Cross Country Ski Canada*, April 13, 2006.
Dusan Grasic: New Farnham Glacier facilities keep national alpine ski racers in Canada, *Alpine Canada*, October 9, 2007.
Mark Greenwald: Alberta advantage rocks Turin Games, Cameron Maxwell, Calgary, February 7, 2006.

WinSport's winning ways
Discussions
Gordon Ritchie

Websites

cbc.ca

Comments made by

Bill France: Calgary's hill to die for: while the battle of Alberta ebbs and flows, what gives Calgary an edge is a precious keepsake of the 1988 Winter Games — Canada Olympic Park, Dan Barnes, *Edmonton Journal*, September 11, 2007.

4   A Klassen Act: Canada's Speed Skating Success Story

Opening discussion

Discussions

Tracy Cameron, Mark Duk

Publications

Largely ignored here, Canada's outstanding speed skaters forge ahead in the pursuit of excellence, Bill Lankhof, *Toronto Sun*, January 23, 2007.

Internal competition

Websites

Speed Skating Canada, International Olympic Committee, Canadian Olympic Committee

Publications

Largely ignored here, Canada's outstanding speed skaters forge ahead in the pursuit of excellence, Bill Lankhof, *Toronto Sun*, January 23, 2007.

The making of a juggernaut

Discussions

Jean Dupre, Jacques Thibault

A winning mindset

Discussions

Jacques Thibault, Mark Greenwald

Websites

Olympic Oval, Speed Skating Canada, University of Calgary

Raising the bar for skaters
Discussions
Mark Greenwald, Jean Dupre, Sean Ireland, Mark Mathies
Websites
Speed Skating Canada, Girls@Play, United States Speed Skating Association
Comments made by
Gregg Planert: Speed Skating Canada announces departure of high performance director, Emery Holmik, Untitled, Press Release Services, April 26, 2006.
Cindy Klassen and Jean Dupre: Coaching shakeup leaves Canada short an ace, Beverly Smith, *Globe and Mail*, May 26, 2008.
Brian Rahill: Largely ignored here, Canada's outstanding speed skaters forge ahead in the pursuit of excellence, Bill Lankhof, *Toronto Sun*, January 23, 2007.
Apolo Anton Ohno: OhnoZone.net, June 5, 2006.

5   Icing on the Cake: Canada's Recipe for Success in Vancouver 2010

Opening discussion
Discussions
Yves Matson, Tristan Goodman, John Furlong

Own the Podium
Discussions
Bob Story
Websites
Canadian Olympic Committee, Own the Podium
Publications
Canada's goal of 25 medals still in reach, Lori Ewing, Canadian Press, February 17, 2006.
Team Canada reaching for the top, Eric Francis, *Calgary Sun*, February 9, 2006.
Canada caps most successful Winter Olympics on road to Vancouver in 2010, Donna Spencer, *Slam Sports*, February 26, 2006.
Comments made by
Chris Rudge: Fan 590 Sportsnet interview.

Alex Gardiner: Canadian Olympic Committee achieves goal of a top-three finish at the 2006 Olympic Winter Games, Podium, Canadian Olympic Committee Newsletter, vol. 4, issue 2, February-March 2006.

Cathy Priestner Allinger: Cindy Klassen Canada's greatest Olympian, Ken MacQueen, *Maclean's*, March 6, 2006.

Chris Rudge: On snow and ice and in water, Canadian athletes excel in 2006, Jim Morris, Canadian Press, December 20, 2006.

Cathy Priestner Allinger: Canada caps most successful Winter Olympics on road to Vancouver in 2010, Donna Spencer, *Slam Sports*, February 26, 2006.

Chris Rudge: Rudge's doctrine puts athletes' concerns at the forefront, James Christie, *Globe and Mail*, July 19, 2003.

Ken Read: Canada already looking onward and upward, James Christie, *Globe and Mail*, February 28, 2006.

Chris Rudge: Team Canada reaching for the top, Eric Francis, *Calgary Sun*, February 9, 2006.

6   The Truth Revealed: The Sorry State of Our Olympic Efforts

Opening discussion
Discussions
Ron Bowker, Daniel Igali

Websites
International Olympic Committee, Canadian Olympic Committee, Wikipedia, Volleyball Canada, Basketball Canada

Publications
Though more nations enter, Winter Games medals remain dominated by exclusive club, Associated Press, ESPN Newswire, February 19, 2006.

Culture or choice?
Discussions
Daniel Igali, Trevino Betty, Graham Hood
Websites
Sport Canada

A system of ineptitude

Discussions

Donovan Bailey, Graham Hood, Russ Anber, Pat Fiacco, Catherine Dunnette, Conrad Leinemann, Martha Henderson, Sherraine Schalm

Websites, television

TSN, CBC News, the star.com, CBC Beijing Olympics

Blame Swimming Canada coach for this catastrophe, thestar.com, November 20, 2004.

Fred Nykamp sues Canadian Soccer Association, Canadian Press, cbcnews.ca, October 16, 2007.

Sherraine Schalm falls short in Beijing, cbc.ca, August 23, 2008.

Comments made by

Colin Linford: CSA president Colin Linford steps down, Canadian Press-TSN.ca, August 27, 2007.

Publications

To the barricades, it's time for a change, Stephen Brunt, *Globe and Mail*, August 29, 2007.

Problems go far beyond swim coach, Alan Maki, *Globe and Mail*, August 20, 2004.

Swim Canada chooses same coach twice, Blair Sanderson, University of Toronto, undated.

Besieged Canada swim coach rationale for mediocrity, Alan Maki, *Globe and Mail*, August 18, 2004.

Comments made by

Michael Grange: How bad off is Basketball Canada, Michael Grange, *Globe and Mail*, September 27, 2007.

Balkanized boards

Discussions

Bob Storey, Randy Starkman, Bill France, Tim Berrett

Websites

WinSport Canada

Publications

Calgary's hill to die for: while the Battle of Alberta ebbs and flows, what gives Calgary an edge is a precious keepsake of the 1988 Winter Games — Canada Olympic Park, Dan Barnes, *Edmonton Journal*, September 11, 2007.

Comments made by

Chris Rudge: World is leaving us behind: COC, Beverly Smith, *Globe and Mail*, August 30, 2004.

7   Purchasing the Podium: Canada's Plans for Improving Olympic Results

Opening discussion
Websites
FISA
Comments made by
Chris Rudge: Canadian Olympic Committee directs additional funding to B.C. athletes, Canadian Olympic Committee, May 12, 2004.
Dr. Roger Jackson: Canadians want to Own the Podium 2010, *Sport Performance Weekly*, Canadian Sport Centre, August 8, 2006.
Comments made by
Clara Hughes: Purchasing the podium, Eric Francis, *Calgary Sun*, February 9, 2006.
Mark Lowry: Canada facing Olympian Task, Steve Simmons, *Toronto Sun*, August 30, 2004.

A cry for help
Comments made by
Chris Rudge and Mark Lowry: Canada facing Olympian Task, Steve Simmons, *Toronto Sun*, August 30, 2004.

Road to Excellence
Websites
Canadian Olympic Committee
Comments made by
Mark Lowry: Canada's Canadian summer sports plan own program to achieve success at upcoming Olympic Games, *Canadian Sport Weekly*, April 17, 2005.
Chris Rudge: Canadian summer sport community unveils plan to increase podium results at upcoming games, Canadian Olympic Committee Press Release, COC website, June 8, 2006.

Fast out of the gates

Websites

Own the Podium, Canadian Olympic Committee, Vancouver 2010, Sport Research Intelligence Sportive (SIRC)

Comments made by

Chris Rudge: The government of Canada supports Road to Excellence, Government of Canada press release, March 2, 2008.

Iain Brambell: Canadian summer sport community unveils plan to increase podium results at upcoming games, Canadian Olympic Committee press release, COC website, June 8, 2006.

Alex Baumann: Right man to steer ship, Dave Stubbs, *National Post*, September 28, 2006.

Chris Rudge: Athletes left out, Bill Lankhof, Sun Media, March 21, 2007.

Sylvie Bernier: COC urges government to follow through on funding recommendation, James Christie, *Globe and Mail*, February 15, 2008.

Alex Baumann: Beijing a benchmark for Alex Baumann and Road to Excellence, Donna Spencer, Canadian Press, August 4, 2008.

There is an I in team

Discussions

Roger Jackson, Adham Sharara, Daniel Igali, Trevino Betty

Websites, television

Badzine, CBC Sports, Sport Canada

Publications

Inspiration for rowers not far off, Rob Longley, Canoe.ca, August 10, 2008.

One man team, Dave Waddell, *Windsor Star*, July 23, 2008.

Comments made by

Andy McInnis: Government on wrong track, Rob Brodie, *Ottawa Sun*, August 3, 2006.

A flawed approach

Discussions

Roger Jackson, Ian Reade, Walt Macnee

Comments made by

Dr. Dan Mason: Gold for gold: Canadian Olympic Committee scheme proposes spending $110 million to earn 35 medals, Phoebe Day, *folio focus*, University of Alberta, February 18, 2005.

Alex Baumann: Baumann's in deep end in new role, Randy Starkman, *Toronto Star*, May 21, 2007.

Money isn't everything

Discussions

Marvin Washington, Ian Reade

Publications

Gold for gold: Canadian Olympic Committee scheme proposes spending $110 million to earn 35 medals, Phoebe Day, *folio focus*, University of Alberta, February 18, 2005.

Comments made by

Kevin Wamsley: Podium program may not be a good idea, Steve Hubrecht, the *Online Reporter*, University of Western Ontario Graduate Program of Journalism, February 22, 2006.

Ian Reade: Gold for gold: Canadian Olympic Committee scheme proposes spending $110 million to earn 35 medals, Phoebe Day, *folio focus*, University of Alberta, February 18, 2005.

8   Who's Driving the Bus? The Leadership Problem

Opening discussion

Discussions

Tracy Cameron

Websites

Sing 365

Comments made by

Michael Chambers: Failure of some Canadian athletes overshadows Olympic performances of others, Jim Morris, *Montreal Gazette*, August 30, 2004.

Paul Henderson: All that Glitters ..., Cam Cole, *National Post*, August 12, 2004.

Sport Canada

Discussions

Stephen Owen

Websites

Sport Canada, Canadian Sport Centre, Blogs Canada E: Group Multi Partisan Political Punditry

Comments made by

Chris Rudge: COC boss calls on PM to take a stand: Rudge says leadership needed, someone's got to say sport is important, James Christie, *Globe and Mail* (reprinted in *Canadian Sport Centre Sport Performance Weekly*, October 18, 2004).

Denis Coderre: Doan should not represent Canada, TSN website, December 22, 2005.

Eric Brewer and Andy Murray: Shane Doan remained classy right until the very end, Canadian Press and TSN website, May 13, 2007.

Ian Gillespie: Reading between the box scores, Ian Gillespie, Blogs Canada E: Group Multi Partisan Political Punditry, March 1, 2005.

Publications

National Post editorial board: The bill of attainder against Shane Doan, Jonathan Kay, *National Post*, May 3, 2007.

The last word: for the most part our politicians seem only too happy to ignore sport; fortunately Ontario has a guy like Jim Watson helping them out, George Gross, *Toronto Sun*, September 20, 2007.

Comments made by

Don Martin: Backbench a better fit for gaffe prone Guergis, Don Martin, *National Post*, March 31, 2008.

Stephen Owen: All that glitters ..., Cam Cole, *National Post*, August 12, 2004.

Peter Van Loan: Van Loan joins Harper's cabinet, Bill Res, the *King Township Sentinel*.

Self-appointed leader

Websites

Canadian Olympic Committee

Publications

How we're failing our athletes, Randy Starkman, *Toronto Star*, September 24, 2000.

Ford prefers to run things his way, Allan Maki, *Globe and Mail*, August 20, 2004.

Comments made by

David Ford: Ford prefers to run things his way, Allan Maki, *Globe and Mail*, August 20, 2004.

An Olympic battle

Discussions

Walt Macnee, e-mail from Jane Roos

Websites

Slam Sports, Blogspot

Comments made by

Adam van Koeverden: Van Koeverden woos CEOs, Jon Cook, *Slam Sports*, November 18, 2004.

Jake Wetzel and Adam van Koeverden: Olympic wrestling with Roos, blogspot.com, February 4, 2006.

Jane Roos: Empty feeling, Alison Korn, *Slam Sports*, April 20, 2007.

Publications

See you in court, fundraiser tells COC, Wayne Scanlon, *Ottawa Citizen*, February 4, 2006.

The Backdoor Marketer, Lisa D'Innocenzo, *Strategy Magazine*, April 19, 2004.

COC lacks Olympic spirit: battle over trademark with See You In ... fund seems petty, Mike Ulmer, *Toronto Sun*, February 4, 2006.

Comments made by

Daniel Igali: See you in court, fundraiser tells COC, Wayne Scanlon, *Ottawa Citizen*, February 4, 2006.

Labatt's Brewery and Mike Patterson: The backdoor marketer, Lisa D'Innocenzo, *Strategy Magazine*, April 19, 2004.

COC Executive: See you in court, fundraiser tells COC, Wayne Scanlon, *Ottawa Citizen*, February 4, 2006.

David Bedford: COC lacks Olympic spirit: battle over trademark with See You In ... fund seems petty, Mike Ulmer, *Toronto Sun*, February 4, 2006.

Lord of sport

Websites

Cool Running, Sport Canada

Comments made by

Ross Outerbridge: Canadians face difficult test at the Commonwealth Games, James Christie (posted on cool running.com March 16, 2006).

Publications

We deserved better TV coverage than we were given, Jason Warick, *Saskatoon StarPhoenix*, September 14, 2007.

Comments made by

Dan Wolfenden: Funding chasm widens: non-Olympic sports to feel fiscal pinch, Alison Korn, *Toronto Sun*, July 13, 2007.

Who is overseeing sport?

Discussions

Alex Baumann, Trevino Betty, Pat Fiacco, Mark Greenwald

Comments made by

Alex Baumann: Sink or swim, Andrew Duffy, *Ottawa Citizen*, July 22, 2007; Baumann makes case for funding, James Christie, *Globe and Mail*, December 8, 2007; Cash for medals not an incentive, Canada's Olympians insist, Bruce Cheadle, Canadian Press, November 19, 2007.

Mark Lowry: Review ordered into Canada's medal woes, Reuters, August 29, 2004.

Stacie Smith: Medals do matter, Jason Fekete, *Calgary Herald*, August 13, 2004.

Ken Read: Corporate Canada, start training for the next Games, Ken Read and Dan Thompson, *Globe and Mail*, September 2, 2004.

9 The Aussie Touch: A Case Study

Opening discussion

Discussions

Mark Duk, Tracy Cameron

Websites

International Olympic Committee, Commonwealth Games Federation

A fall from grace

Publications

Australia's Sporting Success, John Bloomfield, UNSW Press, 2004.

Full court press
Discussions
Pierre Lafontaine
Comments made by
Australian Prime Minister: Australia's Sporting Success, John Bloomfield, UNSW Press, 2004.
Publications
Australia's Sporting Success, John Bloomfield, UNSW Press, 2004.

An enlightened move
Discussions
Alex Baumann, Kurtis MacGillivary
Publications
Australia's Sporting Success, John Bloomfield, UNSW Press, 2004.

The lessons for Canada
Discussions
Marvin Washington
Websites
Canadian Olympic Committee
Publications
Canada badly needs a new Games plan, Matthew Fisher, *Toronto Sun,* September 22, 2000.
Comments made by
coc: Canadian Olympic Committee launches $8.7 million Excellence Fund, February 2003.
Alex Baumann: Questions for Alex Baumann, asked by Scott Haddow, *Northern Life,* Laurentian Media Group, October 25, 2006.
Ken MacQueen: Canada's medal tally at 2004 Athens Games tumbles, Ken MacQueen, *Maclean's,* September 6, 2004.

The importance of leadership
Discussions
Bob Storey, James Christie, Paul Henderson

Websites
Canadian Sport Centre Weekly
Comments made by
Chris Rudge: coc boss calls on PM to take a stand; Rudge says leadership needed; someone's got to say sport is important, James Christie, *Globe and Mail*, taken from *Canadian Sport Centre Sport Performance Weekly*, October 18, 2004.

10 Melting the Ice: Creating a Culture of Sport

Opening discussion
Discussions
Tracy Cameron, Mark Duk, Dale Henwood, Daniel Igali

Winter mythology
Discussions
Marvin Washington, Alex Gardiner
Websites
Speed Skating Canada
Publications
Quebec catches football fever, Graeme Hamilton, *National Post*, September 20, 2003.

A cash cow
Discussions
Marvin Washington
Websites
Unesco
Publications
Podium program may not be a good idea, Steve Hubrecht, the *Online Reporter*, University of Western Ontario Graduate Program of Journalism, February 22, 2006.
Comments made by
Dr. Bruce Kidd: Ministers call for action to increase opportunities in Canadian communities through a designated national sport, physical activity and

recreation infrastructure program, news release, Conference of Ministers Responsible for Sport, Physical Activity and Recreation, Toronto, Ontario, September 28, 2006.

Building from the ground up
Discussions
Ian Bird
Publications
Reshuffle your priorities and play with your kids, Andre Picard, *Globe and Mail*, June 1, 2006.
Some back Participaction's return, despite costs, Gloria Galloway, *Globe and Mail*, June 10, 2006.
Comments made by
Mark Keast: Provincial ministers want feds to invest more in sports, Mark Keast, *Toronto Sun*, September 29, 2006.
Denis Coderre: Some back Participaction's return, despite costs, Gloria Galloway, *Globe and Mail*, June 10, 2006.
Silken Laumann: Reshuffle your priorities and play with your kids, Andre Picard, *Globe and Mail*, June 1, 2006.

Filling the gap
Discussions
John Mills
Websites
Canada Olympic Park, CODA, WinSport Canada
Comments made by
Jim Younker: CODA and Calgary board of education join forces to enhance quality of life amongst Calgary youth, Media Resources, May 25, 2006.
Stephen Owen: All that glitters ..., Cam Cole, *National Post*, August 12, 2004; Don't judge success by medals: minister, Anne Marie Owens, *Calgary Herald*, August 12, 2004.
Michael Chong: Minister Chong — Sport, HaltonHerald.ca, March 9, 2006; Some back Participaction's return, despite costs, Gloria Galloway, *Globe and Mail*, June 10, 2006.

Fixing the infrastructure
Discussions
Pat Fiacco, Todd Simonson
Publications
Lack of good facilities hurts development of future athletes, Murray Campbell,
Globe and Mail, October 3, 2006.
Ontario looks to upgrade sports infrastructure, James Christie, *Globe and Mail*,
April 3, 2007.
Asper sweetens stadium deal for CFL's Blue Bombers, Mary Agnes Welch,
National Post, January 4, 2008.
Comments made by
Karen Pitre: Toronto lacking facilities for elite Olympic athletes, Rob Granatstein,
Toronto Sun, February 21, 2006.
Jim Watson: Ontario looks to upgrade sports infrastructure, James Christie, *Globe and Mail*, April 3, 2007.

Creating a sport culture
Discussions
Marvin Washington
Websites
Sask Sport
Comments made by
Rob Phillip: Canada offers little to rising sport stars, Nicole Teixeira, Excalibur
Online, January 10, 2007.
Publications
Open letter to Henderson and Gross, as published in the *Toronto Sun*.
Gold for gold: Canadian Olympic Committee scheme proposes spending $110
million to earn 35 medals, Phoebe Day, *folio focus*, University of Alberta,
February 18, 2005.
Playing in the bigs, Cameron Aisnworth-Vincze, macleans.ca, November 16, 2007.
Amateur Sports fuels economy, Neil Scott, *Leader-Post*, December 1, 2007.
Comments made by
Kevin Tyler: Gold for gold: Canadian Olympic Committee scheme proposes
spending $110 million to earn 35 medals, Phoebe Day, *folio focus*, University of
Alberta, February 18, 2005.

Brian Williams: Ontario looks to upgrade sports infrastructure, James Christie, *Globe and Mail*, April 3, 2007.

Bob Phillip: Playing in the bigs, Cameron Aisnworth-Vincze, macleans.ca, November 16, 2007.

Marek Glowacki: Canadian track and field coaches hope to keep athletes home, Richard Cairney, *Express*, University of Alberta, August 13, 2001.

11 One-Stop Shopping: Implementing Excellence

Opening discussion
Discussions
Ron Bowker, Jim Christie, Ken Read, Jake Wetzel, Marnie McBean
Publications
Untitled, Stephen Brunt, *Globe and Mail*, August 18, 2004.
Comments made by
Jim Byers: Canada is emerging as an Olympic powerhouse, Marc Sappenfield, *Christian Science Monitor*, February 23, 2006.

"Dammit, let's do things right!"
Discussions
Ken Read, Donovan Bailey, Anne Merklinger, Mike Spracklen
Websites
Alpine Canada
Comments made by
Ken Read: Ski Team on track despite injuries; 2004 was good for Canadian ski racers, Andrew Mitchell, from Alpine Canada website, April 23, 2004.
Marnie McBean: Top athletes need more support, Jonathan Gatehouse, Canadian Encyclopedia website, July 14, 2004.

Publications
Canada aims higher for 2012, James Christie and Alan Maki, *Globe and Mail*, August 22, 2008.
No pain no gain for rowers in race for gold, Randy Starkman, *Toronto Star*, May 11, 2008.

Comments made by

Anne Merklinger: Canada aims higher for 2012, James Christie and Alan Maki, *Globe and Mail*, August 22, 2008.

Jake Wetzel: No pain no gain for rowers in race for gold, Randy Starkman, *Toronto Star*, May 11, 2008.

From fragmentation to unity
Discussions

Alex Baumann, Alex Gardiner, Sherraine Schalm, Martha Henderson, Pierre Lafontaine, Adham Sharara

Websites

Sport Canada, True Sport, Participation, Canadian Association for Health, Physical Education, Recreation, and Dance

Comments made by

Alex Baumann: More funding means more medals: Oly chief, CTV GlobeMedia.ca, April 21, 2007.

Pierre Lafontaine: Swimming World Radio Archive, March 29, 2007.

Alex Baumann: Games will build legacy, Richard Dooley, *Daily News*, February 17, 2007.

Barney Williams: Time's worth more than athlete funds, Barney Williams, *Toronto Star*, May 16, 2006.

Taking coaching seriously
Discussions

Russ Anber, Donovan Bailey, Tom Ponting, Mark Greenwald, Alex Gardiner, Pat Fiacco, Sherraine Schalm, Joshua Riker-Fox, Adham Sharara, Daniel Igali

Websites

Canadian Olympic Committee, Coaching Association of Canada

Publications

Mitchell gets the boot as men's coach, Neil Davidson, *Globe and Mail*, March 28, 2009.

Comments made by

Mark Lowry: COC review of team performance at Athens 2004, press conference.

Pierre Lafontaine: Boss will be on the deck as Lafontaine oversees swim team training camp, Jim Morris, *Slam Sports*, June 17, 2005; Are Olympic medals worth the cost? Randy Starkman, *Toronto Star*, August 16, 2008.

Rick Brennan and Dwayne De Rosario: Soccer world keeps turning, Richard Starnes, *Calgary Herald*, January 3, 2009.

No lack of opportunity
Discussions
Frank King

The payoff for Calgary
Websites
International Olympic Committee / Marketing Matters, CODA, WinSport
Publications
Calgary Olympics leave lasting mark on Canadian sport, Tara Kimura, cbc.ca, December 19, 2006.
Comments made by
Kevin Wamsley and Tara Kimura: Calgary Olympics leave lasting mark on Canadian sport, Tara Kimura, cbc.ca, December 19, 2006.

Will Vancouver learn from Calgary?
Discussions
Gordon Ritchie, Chris Rudge, Alex Baumann
Websites, television
NBC, University of British Columbia

12 The End of Spectator Sports: Getting Canadian Athletes into the Games

Opening discussion
Discussions
Camille Brillon
Comments made by
Robin Williams: Olympic image and the Sydney brand, Olympic.org.

Arbitrary standards

Websites

International Olympic Committee, Canadian Olympic Committee, AthletesCAN, Canadian University Sport

Comments made by

Vanderlei de Lima: Same kilted men disrupted 03 auto race, Associated Press, September 2, 2004.

COC *and Michael Chambers:* Canadian Olympic Committee mid-games press conference, August 22, 2004.

Karen Purdy: COC top 12 criteria, AthletesCAN position paper.

Publications

Olympics: worthy Canadian athletes left at home, Jason Warick, Saskatoon *StarPhoenix*, August 14, 2004.

Comments made by

Bruce Deacon: Athletics: Bruce Deacon comments on Canadian Olympic Committee Athens 2004 standards, RunnersWeb.com, posted August 7, 2004.

Nick Marrone: Olympics: worthy Canadian athletes left at home, Jason Warick, *Saskatoon StarPhoenix*, August 14, 2004.

Cathy Priestner Allinger and Chris Rudge: Prep work: Canada is viewing Turin as dry run for Vancouver, Eric Francis, *Calgary Sun*, February 11, 2005.

Consistent standards

Websites

AthletesCAN

Comments made by

Cindy Ishoy: Canadian riders take pass on Games, Beverley Smith, *Globe and Mail*, January 9, 2008.

The Vancouver factor

Discussions

John Furlong

Websites

Sport Canada, Alpine Canada, Hockey Canada, Petro-Canada

Comments made by

John Furlong: Canada's winter athletes learning to deal with the pressure of 2010, CP Wire. From the *Canadian Sport Centre Performance Weekly*, February 12,

2007 and from Propelling Canadian athletes toward unparalleled podium success, Vancouver 2010 webpage, April 26, 2007.

Publications

Up off the mat, Allan Maki, *Globe and Mail*, April 18, 2008.

Comments made by

Les Gramantik: Olympics chief in cash plea, James Keller, *Toronto Star*, April 20, 2007.

Clive Llewellyn: Up off the mat, Allan Maki, *Globe and Mail*, April 18, 2008.

A kitchen-table system

Websites

Sport Dispute Resolution Centre of Canada

Comments made by

Patrice M. Brunet: Karen Sergerie, claimant vs. WTF Taekwondo Association of Canada (Respondant), Sport Dispute Resolution Centre of Canada Jurisprudence Database, ADR, 03-0027, December 5, 2003.

Michel G. Picher: Megan Poss vs SYNCHRO CANADA (Respondant) and DUBUC, Jessika, LITTLE, Tracy, MCKENNY, Alison, SONG, Jennifer (Affected or Invited Parties), Ordinary Division, Sport Dispute Resolution Centre of Canada Jurisprudence Database, File Number SDRCC 08-0068, February 21, 2008.

Clara Hughes: Canada caps most successful games ever, Donna Spencer, Canadian Press, February 27, 2006.

Nicole Stevenson: Olympics: worthy Canadian athletes left at home, Jason Warick, Saskatoon StarPhoenix, August 14, 2004.

13 Stop the Whining: Sharing the Blame, Heading for Fame

Opening discussion

Discussions

Sherraine MacKay

Publications

Olympic plan seeks $510 million to put Canadians on podium, Jeff Lee, Vancouver Sun, May 1, 2006.

Comments made by

Tonya Verbeek and Chris Rudge: Funding sponsorship good to see: Olympic athletes tell Mike Ulmer corporate sponsorship critical to winning medals, Mike Ulmer, *Toronto Sun*, November 19, 2004.

14 Going Against the Current: Change Must Come from Within

Opening discussion

Discussions

E-mail Simonson / Cameron

Comments made by

Iain Brambell: Executive committee unanimous on calling for increased government funding for summer sport, *Podium*, Canadian Olympic Committee Newsletter, COC, vol. 5, issue 4, April 2007.

The AthletesCAN experiment

Discussions

Ann Peel

Websites

AthletesCAN

Sleeping with the enemy

Discussions

E-mail Johnstone / Peel, e-mail Brambell / Roos, Ann Peel

Publications

Olympics: Worthy Canadian athletes left at home, Jason Warick, *Saskatoon StarPhoenix*, August 14, 2004.

Comments made by

Karen Purdy: Olympics: worthy Canadian athletes left at home, Jason Warick, *Saskatoon StarPhoenix*, August 14, 2004.

Hiding from the hard questions

Discussions

Dominique Vallee, e-mail Johnstone / Peel, Guy Tanguay, Jane Roos

Websites

Sport Dispute Resolution Centre of Canada

Comments made by

Randy Starkman and Dean Boles: How we're failing our athletes, Randy
Starkman, *Toronto Star*, September 24, 2000.

A slippery slope of complacency

Discussions

Rachel Corbett, e-mail Johnstone / Peel, Guy Tanguay, Ann Peel, Dominique Vallee

Websites

Sport Law, AthletesCAN

15 The Olympic Games: Tracy's View

Opening discussion

Discussions

E-mail Simonson / Cameron

16 All for One and One for All: Putting the Fight Back into Our Athletes

A question of marketing

Publications

Super Bowl is overblown cultural event, Bill Reynolds, *Providence Post*, February
1, 2008

A global business

Discussions

Walt Macnee

Fight!

Discussions

Walt Macnee

Websites, television
ESPN Classic
Comments made by
Bob Stewart: We're Olympic class whiners, Bob Stewart, *Kenora Daily Miner and News*, August 26, 2004
Discussions
Walt Macnee
Websites, television
ESPN Classic, MLBPA

Epilogue

Discussions
E-mail Simonson/ Cameron

Index

LaVergne, TN USA
10 September 2009
157372LV00003B/3/P